RATIONAL-EMOTIVE THERAPY:
FUNDAMENTALS AND INNOVATIONS

Rational-Emotive Therapy

Fundamentals and Innovations

Windy Dryden

CROOM HELM
London & Canberra

© 1984 Windy Dryden
Croom Helm Ltd, Provident House, Burrell Row,
Beckenham, Kent BR3 1AT

Croom Helm Australia Pty Ltd, 28 Kembla St.,
Fyshwick, ACT 2609, Australia

British Library Cataloguing in Publication Data

Dryden, Windy
    Rational-emotive therapy.
    1. Rational-emotive psychotherapy
    I. Title
    616.89'14   RC489.R3

    ISBN 0-7099-0848-2

Printed and bound in Great Britain by
Biddles Ltd, Guildford and King's Lynn

CONTENTS

Contents

To Albert Ellis and Richard Wessler:
Fine teachers of Rational-Emotive Therapy
and Cognitive Behaviour Therapy

PREFACE

    I received my original training as a counsel-
ling psychologist at Aston University in 1974/5. I
became well schooled in client-centred therapy and
felt optimistic about the ability of humans to overcome their problems in the context of a warm,
empathic and genuine relationship with me as their
counsellor. I became discouraged partly because my
clients seemed to want more concrete help than I was
providing them, but also because I could see clearly
what was troubling them and felt ungenuine in not
expressing this to them since this was supposed to
be against the principle of client self-directed
learning. Although I was exposed to the writings of
Albert Ellis in 1974/75 and we seriously studied his
work, the general conclusion that we came to about
RET was that arguing and debating with clients was
not quite right and that it might be OK for brash
American clients but it was not to be widely recommended for use with English clients. My own brief
experimentation with RET methods at this time tended
to support this since I got into a blazing row with
one client who told me in no uncertain terms, where
to put my rational arguments.
    Needless to say, my fellow students and I came
to believe in some of the myths about RET and did
not fully understand what Ellis was trying to
communicate. Fortuitously, in 1977 I attended a
day's workshop run by Maxie Maultsby (whose rational
behaviour therapy was seen at that time as being
synonymous with RET) in Suffolk, and became
seriously interested in RET as a therapeutic method
as a result. Later on I attended a week-long
training course at Littledean, Gloucestershire run
by Virginia Anne Church from San Francisco and this
further stimulated my interest. I decided to go to
New York for an intensive ten-week training period

Preface

at the Institute for Rational-Emotive Therapy in the summer of 1978 and later became the first Briton to become a fully accredited rational-emotive therapist and supervisor. I have thus been an advocate of RET for about six years.

The chapters in this book are a collection of my writings on RET from 1979-1983. In Part A, the fundamentals of rational-emotive theory and practice are presented while in Part B my own major contributions to its theory and practice appear. These 'innovations' stem mainly from my clinical work in (a) a university counselling service; (b) a clinic run for a local General Practitioner, (c) a local Marriage Guidance Council and (d) private practice.

This book is dedicated to both Albert Ellis and Richard Wessler who both in their different ways encouraged and stimulated me to think more deeply about RET theory and practice.

In addition, I wish to acknowledge the influence of the following people on my thinking: Aaron T Beck for his work on inferential distortions and collaborative empiricism; Ed Bordin for his theoretical reformulation of the 'therapeutic alliance' concept; John Davis, Marcia Davis and Arnold Lazarus for their thoughts and writings on eclecticism; Richard Nelson-Jones for his model of the counselling psychologist as a decision-maker; and Ruth Wessler for her continued supportive feedback on my clinical work. I also wish to thank Peter Trower and Andrew Casey who collaborated with me on the original publication of Chapter 9.

Finally I wish to thank the following for granting me permission to reprint material; Ballinger; British Journal of Cognitive Psychotherapy; The Counsellor; Family Process; Institute for RET (UK); The Midland Journal of Psychotherapy; New Forum (now retitled 'Changes'); The Journal of the Psychology and Psychotherapy Association; and Rational Living.

Windy Dryden

FOREWORD: WRITTEN BY ALBERT ELLIS

Windy   Dryden's   Rational-Emotive   Therapy:
Fundamentals and Innovations is accurately titled,
in that it covers clearly and directly, nearly all
the fundamentals of rational-emotive theory and
practice.   It nicely brings RET up to date and it
includes several innovations that Dr Dryden has
added to RET that are well worth using and res-
earching and that may become part of its standard
practice.   I am delighted to write an introduction
to this fine theoretical and practical work.
To add to the comprehensiveness of this book,
let me say something about the origins of RET and to
dispel a few of the myths that have already grown up
about it.   Some writers wrongly state that when RET
was originally presented as RT (rational therapy) in
my first formal paper on it, given at the American
Psychological   Association   annual   convention   in
Chicago in September 1956 (Ellis, 1958a), it was
almost entirely cognitive and that I later added
emotive-evocative   and   behavioral-activity   techniques.   Actually, RET was always affective and
behavioral   as   well   as   cognitive,   for   several
reasons:
(1) I had successfully used behavioral methods
on myself, to overcome my fear of public speaking
and social shyness, when I was in my late teens and
early   twenties,   years   before   I   thought   seriously
about becoming a psychologist and psychotherapist
(Ellis, 1972a).
(2) I was influenced in this respect by some of
the   early   writings   of   John   B.   Watson,   his   associates,   and   other   early   behaviorists   (Dunlap,
1932; Jones, 1924; Watson and Raynor, 1920).
(3) While   practicing   psychoanalysis   and
psychoanalytically   oriented   therapy   from   1947   to
1953, I was distinctly critical of orthodox analysis

and wrote several papers against its antiscientific aspects and its passivity (Ellis, 1949, 1950, 1956). Some of my teachers in this connections were Ferenczi (1952) and Alexander and French (1946).

(4) I was a pioneer sex therapist from 1943 onward and even when I used psychoanalysis for understanding and treating problems of anxiety and depression, I employed active-directive homework-assigning methods with my sexually inadequate clients.

(5) I largely came to RET through my interest in philosophy, which had been my hobby from the age of sixteen. My favorite philosophers were not usually armchair intellectuals but activists who applied philosophy to human happiness and who encouraged people to do something to change their misery-creating thinking. I especially found value in the writings of philosophic activists, including Epicurus, Epictetus, Marcus Aurelius, Schopenhauer, Santayana, and Russell. I wrote my baccalaureate thesis on Concord Economics, which dealt with the economic and social philosophies of activist philosophers such as Ralph Waldo Emerson, Henry David Thoreau, Charles Fourier, and Bronson Alcott.

In my first seminal paper on RET (Ellis, 1958a), I mainly focused on its cognitive and philosophic aspects because I wanted to highlight its differences from the popular therapies of that day - particularly the passive Freudian and Rogerian therapies. But when the use of the name rational therapy led some critics to falsely accuse me of being an eighteenth century rationalist, I changed the name of RT to RET in 1961 (Ellis and Harper, 1961) and began to write more about the emotive and behavioral aspects of RET (Ellis, 1962). I also tried to make clear the RET interactional view of cognition, emotion, and behavior, and in Reason and Emotion in Psychotherapy restated my original (Ellis, 1958a) position as follows:

"The theoretical foundations of RT are based on the assumption that human thinking and emotion are not two disparate or different processes, but that they significantly overlap and are in some respects, for all practical purposes, essentially the same thing. Like the other two basic life processes, sensing and moving, they are integrally interrelated and never can be seen wholly apart from each other.

In other words: none of the four fundamental life operations - sensing, moving, emoting, and thinking, is experienced in isolation. If

an individual senses something (e.g. , sees a
stick) he also tends, at the very same time, to
do something about it (pick it up, kick it, or
throw it away), to have some feeling about it
(like it or dislike it), and to think about it
(remember seeing it previously or imagine what
he can do with it). Similarly, if he acts,
emotes, or thinks, he also consciously or un-
consciously involves himself in the other
behavior processes" (Ellis, 1962, pp. 38-39).
RET, then, has always been and still remains
integrational and multimodal. It is a comprehensive
system of psychotherapy based on several theories of
human behavior and of behavioral change; and it
strives to state its basic theoretical constructs in
testable ways (Ellis, 1962, 1973, 1984; Ellis and
Whiteley, 1979). Because its theories are relatively simple, direct, and clear, they have been
subjected to literally hundreds of controlled
scientific experiments that have largely tended to
support them (DiGiuseppe, Miller, and Trexler,
1979; Ellis, 1979a, 1984; McGovern, 1983).
     In addition to being comprised of testable
theories, RET is also eclectic in its use of
therapeutic techniques and uses a greater variety of
such techniques than virtually any other major form
of therapy; and it is only rivaled in this respect
by a few systems, such as multimodal therapy
(Lazarus, 1981), which stresses technical eclecticism and omits RET's theoretical formulations.
Moreover, although RET uses many different kinds of
cognitive, affective, and behavioral methods to
obtain practical results, it favors certain ones as
being more "efficient" and "elegant" than others and
it emphasizes clients' making a profound attitudinal or philosophic change rather than mainly
ridding themselves of their presenting symptoms
(Ellis, 1979a, 1980a, 1980b).
     What are some of RET's unique features? Windy
Dryden has competently dealt with many of them in
the pages of this book but let me give my own
summary. Although what I call general RET is
virtually synonymous with cognitive-behavior
therapy, preferential RET (which its practitioners
use whenever feasible but not whenever possible)
includes the following main features.
     (1) It is highly interactional, as noted
above. First, cognitions, emotions, and behaviors
are never considered monolithically but as including and transacting with each other. Second,
the famous ABCs of RET are also seen as interacting

with and partially including one another. A stands
for Activating events or experiences; or for stimuli
impinging on humans. B stands for Beliefs - that
is, ideas, inferences, and evaluations about As. C
stands for cognitive, emotive, and behavioral Consequences of A times B. Although simple RET teaches
clients that Activating Events (As) precede and seem
to "cause" emotional and behavioral Consequences
(Cs) - e.g., you treat me unjustly at A and your
unfairness "causes" my feelings of anger at C - the
more direct and more important "cause" of C is B -my
Beliefs that you must not treat me unjustly and that
you are a louse when you do - more complex (and more
accurate) RET accepts the reality that A partially
includes B and C. Thus, you treat me "unjustly" at
A partly because I see your behavior as "unjust" and
I feel that I "need" you to treat me justly.
Similarly, B (my Belief that you must not treat me
unjustly) partly includes my observation of your
(and others') unjust behavior and includes my desire
to be treated justly; and C (my anger at you for
treating me "unjustly" to a considerable degree incorporates the Activating event (how you behaved
toward me) and my Belief system (that you must treat
me fairly). A, B, and C, then are seen in RET as
somewhat distinct from each other but as also including the other two concepts.

(2) RET holds that peple can easily pick up
irrational Beliefs (iBs) that lead to disturbed
Consequences from their parents, teachers, and
others (e.g., superstitions like "I must have good
luck, but now that I broke this mirror I will surely
have bad luck") but this is partly because they are
born with a tendency to think in this irrational
manner themselves and therefore accept others' irrationalities.   More importantly, people learn
family and cultural standards, which are often quite
rational (e.g., "I preferably had better treat
others considerately and politely if I want to get
along with them") and then activate their own innate
tendency to overgeneralise and to turn these
standards into irrational Beliefs (iBs) (e.g.,
"Because it is important for me to get along with
others and to treat them considerately and politely,
I have to do so at all times and must do so
perfectly; else I am a totally unlovable, worthless
person!"). Even if we had the most rational up-
bringing, virtually all humans would often take
their individual and social preferences and irrationally escalate them into absolutistic demands

on (a) themselves, (b) other people, and (c) the universe around them (Ellis, 1962, 1971a, 1973, 1976, 1984).

(4) Humans are so uniquely involved in cognitive processes (by nature as well as by social learning) that they continually use them to instigate, change, and chain their emotional and behavioral reactions. When they feel and behave, they almost always have some thoughts <u>about</u> their feelings and actions; and these thoughts lead them to have other feelings and behaviors. Thus, when they feel sad about, say, the loss of a loved one, they usually <u>see</u> or <u>observe</u> or <u>realize</u> that they are sad, evaluate this feeling (e.g., "Isn't it good that I am sad because this proves how much I really loved the person I lost" or "Isn't it bad that I am sad because this shows that I am letting myself be too deeply affected").

When people feel emotionally disturbed at C - that is, feel seriously anxious, depressed, self-downing, or hostile - they quite frequently view their symptoms absolutistically and awfulizingly and thereby irrationally conclude: "I <u>should</u> not, <u>must</u> not be depressed! How <u>awful</u> that <u>I feel</u> this <u>way!</u> I <u>can't stand it!</u> What <u>a fool I am</u> for giving in to this feeling!" They then develop a secondary symptom - depression about depression or anxiety about anxiety - that may be more severe and more incapacitating than their primary symptom and that may prevent them from understanding and working against their primary disturbance. RET especially looks for their secondary symptoms and usually deals with these before the therapist works too hard to help people with their primary symptoms, because it has found that this is normally the most efficient process of treatment (Ellis, 1962, 1979b, 1980c).

(5) Some psychologists, such as Zajonc (1980), distinguish between "cold" and "hot" cognitions; and RET goes one step further and distinguishes among cold, warm, and hot cognitions: (a) Cold cognitions are largely observations, descriptions, and nonevaluative inferences and conclusions: such as, "I am going for a job interview tomorrow", "This interview will probably include some difficult questions", and "If I don't get this job I will look for another one". Cold cognitions result in few or no emotional states. (b) Warm cognitions are evaluations of what goes on in people's lives but tend to emphasize preferences and nonpreferences rather than commands and necessities. For example: "If the job interview includes some difficult

questions, I won't like it", "If I fail the interview and don't get offered the job, that will be
bad", "If I don't get a job for a long period of
time, that will be very bad". (c) Hot cognitions
are evaluations of what happens to people but tend
to emphasize commands and necessities rather than
preferences. For example: "I must pass this job
interview and get offered the job, for that would be
terrible if I failed!" "If I don't get this job and
am out of work for a long time, that will mean that
I am no good as a worker and am an undeserving,
rotten person!" Warm cognitions lead to (mild or
intense) emotions, such as feelings of concern,
regret, sorrow, frustration, annoyance, pleasure,
and satisfaction. Hot cognitions tend to lead to
(mild or intense) feelings of disturbance, such as
severe feelings of anxiety, depression, inadequacy,
rage, grandiosity, and manic states. RET special-
izes in showing people how to distinguish their
cold, warm, and hot cognitions; how to connect them
with the kinds of feelings (or nonfeelings) they
experience; and how to change them when they help to
create emotional disturbances.

(6) RET rarely tries to change people's warm
cognitions - their desires, goals, purposes, and
values, nor the "appropriate" (that is self-
helping) emotions to which they tend to lead. Thus,
if they strongly want a job and are rejected for it,
we assume that their desire for it is probably valid
and that the thwarting of this desire will often
lead to appropriate feelings of disappointment and
frustration and to self-helping behaviors of
continued efforts to look for another job. Negative
feelings like disappointment, frustration, annoyance, irritation, sorrow, and regret are usually
considered to be healthy in RET and no effort is
made to change them.

If, however, people strongly insist that they
must get accepted for every job they want, and if
they thereby transform their desires into absolutistic commands and demands, RETers assume that
their unconditional shoulds and musts are irrational, illegitimate, and invalid because they
will usually (not always) lead to inappropriate
feelings of anxiety and/or depression and to dysfunctional behaviors, such as procrastinating on
looking for other jobs. RET, therefore, attempts to
change these (dangerously) hot cognitions into warm
evaluations - or into wishes and preferences.

(7) RET, again, acknowledges that people have
many different kinds of Beliefs, cognitions, or

ideas. For the most part, these are placed under the heading of B (Beliefs) in RET theory and practice; but some writers put some of them under A (Wessler and Wessler, 1980). In the diagnosis and treatment of emotional disturbance, I usually place them under B and put them in the following sub-categories: (a) Nonevaluative observations or descriptions of what is happening to or with clients. Examples: "I see that my job interviewer gave me a short interview". "I was told that the company that interviewed me would get in touch with me within the next two weeks". (b) Nonevaluative inferences about what is happening. Examples: "Because the job interviewer gave me a short interview that may mean that I will not get the job". "Because the company that interviewed me told me that they would get in touch with me within a few weeks and did not hire me immediately that may mean that they are interviewing other candidates for the job". (c) Evaluative nonabsolutistic inferences about what is happening. Example: "Because the job interviewer gave me a short interview, that surely means that he doesn't like me and that I will not get that job and may not get many similar jobs. I don't like that fact and, if it turns out to be true, that would be unfortunate". (d) Evaluative necessitous inferences and conclusions about what is happening. Examples: "Because I must get the job for which I interviewed, and there is a good chance that I will not get it, that is awful and proves that I am a rotten person!" "Because it is necessary that I get all the jobs that I apply for and because it looks like I will not get this one, I will never be able to get any good job and will be an unemployed, worthless individual for the rest of my life!"

RET is interested in all the important Beliefs (Bs) that people may have about Activating Events (As) in their life; but it particularly focuses on their evaluative preferential inferences and upon their evaluative necessitous inferences and con-clusions about these As.

(8) RET assumes that the most important and basic irrational Beliefs (iBs) that people use or create to make themselves emotionally disturbed and behaviorally dysfunctional are their absolutistic or unconditional shoulds and musts. Thus, they devoutly believe: "Under all conditions, no matter what, I have to succeed at obtaining all the jobs in which I am really interested". RET assumes that the probability is very high that whenever people are

neurotically disturbed (e.g., seriously anxious or depressed), they are not merely strongly <u>preferring</u> to succeed at some task and/or to be approved by others for succeeding, but that they are also explicitly or implicitly <u>demanding</u> or <u>commanding</u> that they absolutely <u>must</u> succeed and/or be approved. RET's cardinal rule to understand the main (though not the <u>only</u>) source of human disturbance, therefore, is: Cherchez <u>le should</u>, cherchez <u>le must</u>; look for the unconditional should, look for the absolutistic must.

(9) RET assumes that when people disturb themselves by strongly holding absolutistic shoulds and musts they almost inevitably create one, two, or three concomitant disturbing Beliefs: (a) <u>Awfulizing</u>: "Because I <u>must</u> do well on this job interview and have not done as well as I <u>have to</u> do, it is awful, terrible, and horrible!" (b) <u>I-can't-stand-it-itis</u>: "Because I lost this job by not doing as well in the job interview as I <u>should</u> have done, I can't bear it, can't tolerate it, and my life is and will remain almost totally miserable!" (c) <u>Self-damnation</u>: "When I don't do as well at getting jobs as I <u>must</u> do I am a <u>rotten job-seeker</u> and a <u>bad, worthless person</u> who doesn't <u>deserve</u> good things!"

RET theory says that these three common irrational Beliefs (iBs) mainly follow from explicit or implicit musts and would rarely exist if humans <u>only</u> rigorously stayed with their preferences. For if people believe, "I would very much <u>prefer</u> to pass this interview and get this job, but I never <u>have to</u> get my preference fulfilled", they would <u>seldom</u> conclude, "It's awful when I fail!" "I can't stand it!" and "I am a bad person for failing!" They still <u>could</u> make these conclusions without musturbatory premises but they probably rarely would.

Awfulizing and musturbating can be reciprocally influential. Just as people say to themselves, "I <u>must</u> succeed and it is therefore <u>awful</u> when I fail", they can also tell themselves, "<u>It's awful</u> when I fail, therefore I <u>must</u> succeed." Mostly, they seem to start with a strong (overt or covert) philosophy of musts and thereby get into awfulizing; but sometimes they may do the reverse. RET assumes that the musts are usually basic and that if people can be shown how to surrender unconditional shoulds, oughts, musts, and necessities and only retain desires, wishes, and preferences, they will rarely disturb themselves emotionally but will merely feel sad and frustrated when they do not get what they prefer.

(10) Human cognitions include a large number of other irrationalities, in addition to those that seem most involved with emotional disturbance; and these are probably mainly contributed to or "caused" by innate human tendencies to think and to infer crookedly (Ellis, 1962; Kahneman and Tversky, 1973; Nisbett and Ross, 1980); Tversky and Kahneman, 1971, 1981). Most of these congitive irrationalities do not often seem to lead to disturbance; but as Ellis (1962, 1971c, 1973, 1984; Ellis and Harper, 1961, 1975), Beck (Beck, Rush, Shaw and Emery, 1979), and Burns (1980) have shown, several of them commonly do. Thus, people disturb themselves by over-generalizing, catastrophizing, magnification, non-sequiturs, unrealistic thinking, labeling, all or nothing thinking, and personalizing. Although these many kinds of irrational and illogical cog-nitions exist in their own right (as part of the human condition) and although they lead to much inefficiency and human harm, RET holds that when they create emotional disturbances they usually relate to hot, evaluative necessitous thinking and tend to stem from or be allied to absolutistic musts.

Thus, when people fail to get a job they can tell themselves, "I am a total failure" (all or nothing thinking), "I shall never be able to get a good job" (overgeneralization), "This is the end of the world!" (catastrophizing), "This proves I am a loser!" (labeling), and "They refused to hire me because they know there's something really rotten about me!" (personalization). These are all un-realistic or antiempirical statements - because there is no real evidence to sustain them and they are most probably factually false. In most kinds of cognitive therapy - e.g., that of Beck (1976), Maultsby (1975), Meichenbaum (1977), and Wessler (1982) - they would be realistically and logically disputed by questioning their empirical validity.

In RET, this would also be done. But it would be assumed that these irrationalities largely stem from some basic philosophic musts, such as: "Because I must perform outstandingly well in job-seeking situations, and because I should have ob-tained this particular job by having a great inter-view and by marvelously impressing my prospective employers, therefore I am a total failure, therefore I'll never be able to get a good job, therefore this is the end of the world, therefore this proves that

I am a loser, and <u>therefore</u> they refused to hire me because they know <u>there is</u> something really rotten about me!" RET, then, usually assumes that the musturbatory thinking of people who are disturbed about not getting a job is fundamental and basic and that without it they would less frequently resort to antiempirical irrational self-statements. So, in addition to showing these individuals how to be more realistic, RET reveals to them their underlying musturbatory philosophies and tries to help them surrender these, too.

(11) Unlike other therapies - including most cognitive-behavioral psychotherapies -RET not only actively disputes people's irrational Beliefs (iBs) and provides them with alternative rational or coping statements, but when they are capable of learning the rudiments of the scientific method it tries to teach them these rudiments: so that, subsequent to therapy, they can <u>themselves</u> look for, discover, and counterattack <u>their</u> unrealistic and musturbatory irrationalities that lead to disturbance. Where feasible, RET tries to help people <u>internalize</u> the scientific method and to use it to <u>solve their</u> own emotional and behavioral problems for the rest of their lives. It hopes that they will, during <u>and</u> after therapy, adopt flexible, undogmatic, <u>empir</u>ically-oriented modes of thinking that, it assumes, constitute the essence of emotional health (Ellis, 1983a), and it tries to teach clients that it is preferable that they use RET effectively but that there is no reason why they <u>must</u>!

(12) RET is one of the few schools of therapy that doesn't espouse self-esteem but that tries to help people refuse to rate their "selves", their totality, their essence, or their being <u>at all</u> - but only to rate their acts, deeds, and performances. It tries to eliminate ego-evaluation and to help people <u>be</u> and <u>enjoy</u> rather than to <u>prove</u> themselves (Ellis, 1972a, 1973, 1984).

(13) RET is humanistic - indeed, doubly humanistic - in that it (a) attempts to help people maximize their individuality, freedom, self-interest, and self-control at the same time that it (b) tries to help them live in an involved, committed, and selectively loving manner with other humans. It thereby strives to facilitate individual <u>and</u> social interest (Adler, 1964; Ellis, 1973, 1984; <u>Ell</u>is and Becker, 1982). Unlike some of the other cognitive-behavior therapies, RET allies itself with a humanistic-existentialist outlook. It

focuses mainly on human survival and happiness
rather than on any absolutistic or authoritarian
world order or on supernatural dictates. It views
and accepts all humans as human, never as either
subhuman or superhuman. It emphasizes (though never
deifies) will and choice rather than rigid deter-
minism or fate in human affairs (Ellis, 1972b, 1973,
1984).

(14) RET encourages therapist-client empathy
and collaborative relationship; and it notably emphasizes therapists' giving their clients unconditional acceptance or what Rogers (1961) calls
unconditional positive regard, no matter how badly
they behave inside and outside the therapy sessions
(Ellis, 1962, 1971, 1972b, 1973, 1984). It promotes
active listening and revolving discussion sequence
by both therapists and clients (Crawford, 1982).
But it opposes therapists unethically indulging
themselves in order to enjoy therapy sessions at
their clients' expense (Ellis, 1983b). And it
stresses the importance of therapists' serving as
effective authoritative (not authoritarian!) encouraging teachers - who are not unduly warm or
reinforcing to clients and who avoid making them
dependent and concomitantly avoid strengthening
their dire need for approval (Ellis, 1983b). RET
practitioners also encourage and push clients to
face and accept reality and often actively persuade
them to go through pain to get gain (Ellis and
Knaus, 1977).

(15) RET is notably emotive in that it holds
that disturbed individuals powerfully and vigorously create and maintain irrational Beliefs,
neurotic feelings, and dysfunctional behaviors and
that they therefore had better forcefully, dram-
atically, and affectively change their thoughts,
emotions, and behaviors (Ellis, 1969, 1971b, 1984;
Ellis and Abrahms, 1978). Because they easily and
naturally disturb themselves and have done so for
many years, they had better strongly and evocatively
work at modifying their conduct. Consequently, RET
almost always uses a number of emotive-evocative
techniques (e.g., rational-emotive imagery, shame
attacking exercises, and strong self-statements) to
help clients change (Ellis and Abrahms, 1978).

(16) RET espouses individual and group therapy
but also believes in psychoeducational methods that
can be used to supplement and enhance these kinds of
therapy or that can be used in themselves as self-
help devices. It therefore actively promotes the
distribution and use of many RET-oriented pamphlets

and books, such as How to Live with a "Neurotic" (Ellis, 1957), Sex Without Guilt (Ellis, 1958b), Humanistic Psychotherapy: The Rational-Emotive Approach (Ellis, 1973), A New Guide to Rational Living (Ellis and Harper, 1975), Overcoming Procrastination (Ellis and Knaus, 1977), and A Guide to Personal Happiness (Ellis and Becker, 1982). It also encourages the use, by clients and others, of many audio visual aids, such as Conquering the Dire Need for Love (Ellis, 1974a), Conquering Low Frustration Tolerance (Ellis, 1974b), How to Stubbornly Refuse to be Ashamed of Anything (Ellis, 1971b), I'd Like to Stop But . . . (Ellis, 1974c), Self-hypnosis: The Rational-Emotive Approach (Golden, 1983), and Twenty-one Ways to Stop Worrying (Ellis, 1971c). RET also sponsors many courses, workshops, and seminars for clients and for members of the public, through which they can pick up some of the main elements of RET through psycho-educational procedures.

(17) While RET is strong on using many behavioral and emotive, as well as many cognitive, techniques, it is also distinctly selective and not merely purely eclectic in the methods it usually employs. Thus, it avoids (though not absolutist-ically avoids) using these procedures: (a) Those that help people become more dependent (e.g., the creation of a transference neurosis and the use of therapist warmth as a strong reinforcer). (b) Those that help people become more gullible and suggestible (e.g., certain kinds of positive thinking and polyannaism). (c) Those that are longwinded and inefficient (e.g., psychoanalytic methods in general and free association in particular). (d) Those that help people feel better rather than to get better (e.g., some experiential techniques like fully expressing one's feelings). (e) Those that have dubious validity (e.g., neurolinguistic programming). (f) Those that include an anti-scientific philosophy (e.g., faith healing and mysticism). (g) Those that are harmful to a good number of clients (e.g., encouraging clients, as in Gestalt and Primal therapy, to explosively express their anger).

(18) RET holds that people, as they learn to gradually work at giving up their phobias, obsessions, and compulsions, frequently sink right back into these behaviors and that if they implosively work at surrendering them (e.g., by using implosive or massed in vivo desensitization) they will tend to change more quickly and effectively,

with fewer retrogressions. It therefore often favors implosive homework assignments, although it does not insist that all clients use this method.

(19) RET theorizes (on the basis of much clinical experience and a number of controlled studies) that difficult clients frequently will not change their behavior by using reinforcements because they so stubbornly stick to their inappropriate feelings that normal reinforcements will not induce them to change their hedonic calculus and to give up certain highly pleasureable pursuits (e.g., smoking or gambling) for what they view as lesser pleasures (e.g., listening to music or looking at television). These same clients, however, will sometimes do almost anything to avoid stiff penalties (e.g., lighting each cigarette with a ten dollar bill). So RET practitioners often contract with such difficult clients that they give themselves a severe disadvantage (not including self-damnation) every time they fail to do what they promise themselves to do or insist on doing what they promise themselves not to do (Ellis, 1974b, 1984; Ellis and Abrahms, 1978).

(20) Although many RETers use standard assessment procedures, RET theorizes that many of these (e.g., Rorschach and TAT evaluations) are fairly useless when employed with therapy clients; and that even the more useful ones (e.g., the MMPI and the Beck Depression Inventory) provide information that can often more accurately be obtained by using the therapeutic process as a means of diagnosis. Particularly when a therapist ferrets out the ABCs of RET and actively and quickly begins to Dispute (at D) clients' irrational Beliefs (iBs), he or she is more likely to discover how severely disturbed these clients are and what is their prognosis than when this therapist employs other assessment procedures. So RET emphasizes active-directive therapy as diagnosis.

(21) RET, more than virtually any other system of therapy, looks for both ego-anxiety (e.g., "I am an inadequate and rotten person if I fail and lose others' approval") and discomfort anxiety or low frustration tolerance (e.g., "I need what I want when I want it and the world and my existence is no good if life gives me more hassles than it should!"). It also looks for secondary symptoms, such as discomfort anxiety about ego anxiety and ego anxiety about discomfort anxiety (e.g., "I am a bad person because I have low frustration tolerance and do not get off my rump to change it!"). RET

emphasizes ameliorating both ego-based and low frustration-based disturbances (Ellis, 1979b, 1980c, 1984 and goes beyond most other therapies in this respect.

(22) RET largely endorses the Freudian view of human defensiveness (A. Freud, 1937); and it partly goes along with Berne's (1964) notion of people's using payoffs when they refuse to give up their disturbances. But it holds that many psychological defences (e.g., rationalization and avoidance) are created to ward off self-downing (ego-anxiety) and can be minimized by helping clients to achieve complete self-acceptance, no matter how they perform or who does or does not approve of them. It also holds that, instead of being dramatic and clever, as Berne often alleges, many payoffs consist of the undramatic feelings of comfort and ease that people receive from refusing to take the trouble of changing (Ellis and Whiteley, 1979).

I could continue to list the distinctive features of RET but this Introduction to Windy Dryden's book is meant to be just that - and is not designed to be exhaustive. Besides, the book itself consistently shows how rational-emotive therapy differs from other - including other cognitive-behavioral - therapies; and it does so in lucid detail.

What are the distinctive features of Rational--Emotive Therapy: Fundamentals and Innovations? What are some of the original contributions to RET that Dr Dryden has made in this book? Without trying too hard, I can think of several:

* He has reviewed the distinctive attributes of RET and skillfully compared them to those of other leading psychotherapies.
* He has given his own amalgamated version of cognitive-behavior therapy, endorsing certain aspects of it and modifying other aspects, in accordance with his own clinical experience.
* He writes as an incisive theoretician as well as a highly practical and down-to-earth counsellor.
* He has importantly expanded some of the ideas on the issue of force and energy in RET (Ellis, 1979c) and has come up with a valuable presentation of what he calls "Vivid RET".
* He has gone beyond the usual RET formulations about achieving an effective therapeutic alliance (Bard, 1980; Ellis,

1973; Ellis and Whiteley, 1979; Walen, DiGiuseppe and Wessler, 1980; Wessler and Wessler, 1980) and has made original contributions in this area.

* He has, from his vantage point as a social (as well as a counselling) psychologist, augmented RET with some important sociological considerations.
* He has, following the earlier example of one of the most prominent RETers, Dr Robert A. Harper, emphasized the importance of eclecticism in rational-emotive therapy.
* He has amplified RET's approach to social skills training and to marital therapy.
* He has presented an original model of audiotape supervision by mail that can prove exceptionally helpful to almost any RET supervisor who uses this modality.

In these and many other ways Windy Dryden has added his own unique imprint to some of the most influential theories and practices of RET. Once again, then, I am delighted to endorse his book and to hope that this Introduction will persuade many RET practitioners and aficionados as well as therapists from other orientations to read it. The probability that they will greatly benefit from doing so is, I hypothesize, very high!

Albert Ellis, PhD
Institute for Rational-Emotive Therapy
45 East 65th Street
New York, NY 10021
USA

Foreword

REFERENCES

Adler, A. Superiority and social interest.
    Evanston, IL.: Northwestern University
    Press, 1964.
Alexander, F., and French, T.M. Psychoanalytic
    therapy. New York: Ronald, 1946.
Bard, J. Rational-emotive therapy in practice.
    Champaign, IL.: Research Press, 1980.
Beck, A.T. Cognitive therapy and the emotional
    disorders. New York: International Univ-
    ersities Press, 1976.
Beck, A.T., Rush, A.J., Shaw, B.F., and Emery, G.
    Cognitive therapy of depression. New York:
    Guilford, 1979.
Berne, E. Games people play. New York: Grove,
    1964.
Burns, D.D. Feeling good. New York: Morrow,
    1980.
Crawford, T. Communication and rational-emotive
    therapy. Paper presented in Los Angeles,
    October, 1982.
DiGiuseppe, R.A., Miller, N.J., and Trexler,
    L.D. A review of rational-emotive psycho-
    therapy outcome studies. In A. Ellis and
    J.M. Whiteley (Eds.), Theoretical and
    empirical foundations of rational-emotive
    therapy. Monterey, CA.: Brooks/Cole,
    1979.
Dunlap, K. Habits: Their making and unmaking.
    New York: Liveright 1932.
Ellis, A. Towards the improvement of psycho-
    analytic research. Psychoanalytic Review,
    1949, 36, 123-143.
Ellis, A. An introduction to the scientific
    principles of psychoanalysis. Provincetown,
    Mass.: Journal Press, 1950.

Ellis, A. An operational reformulation of some
of the basic principles of psychoanalysis.
Psychoanalytic Review, 1956, 43, 163-180.
Also in H. Feigl and M. Scriven (Eds.),
Minnesota studies in the philosophy of
science, Vol. I. Minneapolis: University
Press, 1956.

Ellis, A. How to live with a "neurotic". New
York: Crown, 1957. Rev. ed., North Hollywood:
Wilshire, 1975.

Ellis, A. Rational psychotherapy. Journal
of General Psychology, 1958, 59, 35-49.
(a)

Ellis, A. Sex without guilt. Secaucus, N.J.:
Lyle Stuart, 1958. Rev. ed.: Hollywood:
Wilshire, 1965. (b)

Ellis, A. Reason and emotion in psychotherapy.
Secaucus, N.J.: Lyle Stuart, 1962.

Ellis, A. A weekend of rational encounter.
In A. Burton (Ed.), Encounter. San Francisco:
Jossey-Bass, 1969.

Ellis, A. Growth through reason. North Hollywood:
Wilshire, 1971. (a)

Ellis, A. How to stubbornly refuse to be ashamed
of anything. Cassette recording. New
York: Institute for Rational-Emotive Therapy,
1971. (b)

Ellis, A. Twenty-one ways to stop worrying.
Cassette recording. New York: Institute
for Rational-Emotive Therapy, 1971. (c)

Ellis, A. Psychotherapy without tears. In
A. Burton (Ed.), Twelve therapists. San
Francisco: Jossey-Bass, 1972. (a)

Ellis, A. Psychotherapy and the value of a
human being. New York: Institute for
Rational-Emotive Therapy, 1972. (b)

Ellis, A. Humanistic psychotherapy: The rational-
emotive approach. New York: Crown, 1973.

Ellis, A. Conquering the dire need for love.
Cassette recording. New York: Institute
for Rational-Emotive Therapy, 1974. (a)

Ellis, A. Conquering low frustration tolerance.
Cassette recording. New York: Institute
for Rational Emotive Therapy, 1974. (b)

Ellis, A. I'd like to stop but . . . Conquering
addictions. Cassette recording. New
York: Institute for Rational-Emotive Therapy,
1974. (c)

Ellis, A. The biological basis of human irrationality. _Journal of Individual Psychology_, 1976, _32_, 145-168. Also: New York: Institute for Rational-Emotive Therapy, 1976.

Ellis, A. Rational-emotive therapy: Research data that support the clinical and personality hypotheses of RET and other modes of cognitive-behavior therapy. In A. Ellis and J.M. Whiteley (Eds.), _Theoretical and empirical foundations of rational-emotive therapy_. Monterey, CA: Brooks/Cole, 1979. (a)

Ellis, A. Discomfort anxiety: A new cognitive behavioral construct. Part 1. _Rational Living_, 1979, _14(2)_, 3-8. (b)

Ellis, A. The issue of force and energy in behavioral change. _Jounal of Contemporary Psychotherapy_, 1979, _10_, 83-97. (c)

Ellis, A. Rational-emotive therapy and cognitive behavior therapy: Similarities and differences. _Cognitive Therapy and Research_, 1980, _4_, 325-340. (a)

Ellis, A. The value of efficiency in psychotherapy. _Psychotherapy: Theory, Research and Practice_, 1980, _17_, 414-419. (b)

Ellis, A. Discomfort anxiety: A new cognitive behavioral construct. Part 2. _Rational Living_, 1980, _15(1)_, 25-30. (c)

Ellis, A. _The case against religiosity_. New York: Institute for Rational-Emotive Therapy, 1983. (a)

Ellis, A. The philosophical implications and dangers of some popular behavior therapy techniques. In M. Rosenbaum, C.M. Franks, and Y. Jaffe (Eds.), _Perspectives on behavior therapy in the eighties_. New York: Springer, 1983. (b)

Ellis, A. _Rational-emotive therapy and cognitive behavior therapy_. New York: Springer, 1984.

Ellis, A., and Abrahms, E. _Brief psychotherapy in medical and health practice_. New York: Springer, 1978.

Ellis, A., and Becker, I. _A guide to personal happiness_. North Hollywood: Wilshire, 1982.

Ellis, A., and Harper, R.A. _A guide to rational living_. Englewood Cliffs, N.J.: Prentice-Hall, 1961.

Ellis, A., and Harper, R.A. _A new guide to rational living_. North Hollywood: Wilshire, 1975.

Ellis, A., and Knaus, W. Overcoming procrastin-
    ation. New York: New American library,
    1977.
Ellis, A., and Whiteley, J.M. Theoretical and
    empirical foundations of rational-emotive
    therapy. Monterey, CA: Brooks/Cole, 1979.
Ferenczi, S. Further contributions to the tech-
    nique of psychoanalysis. New York: Basic
    Books, 1952.
Freud, A. The ego and the mechanisms of defense.
    London: Hogarth, 1937.
Golden, W. Self-hypnosis: The rational-emotive
    approach. Cassette recording. New York:
    Institute for Rational-Emotive Therapy,
    1983.
Jones, M.C. The elimination of children's fears.
    Journal of Experimental Psychology, 1924,
    7, 383-390. (a)
Jones, M.C. A laboratory study of fear: the
    case of Peter. Journal of Genetic Psychology,
    1924, 31, 308-315. (b)
Kahneman, D., and Tversky, A. On the psychology
    of prediction. Psychological Review, 1973,
    80, 237-250.
Lazarus, A.A. The practice of multimodal therapy.
    New York: McGraw-Hill, 1981.
Maultsby, M.C., Jr. Help yourself to happniess.
    New York: Institute for Rational-Emotive
    Therapy, 1975.
McGovern, T. A review of outcome studies of
    rational-emotive therapy: 1977-1981.
    M.A. Thesis, Loyola University of Chicago,
    1983.
Meichenbaum, D. Cognitive behavior modification.
    New York: Plenum, 1977.
Nisbett, R., and Ross, L. Human inference:
    Strategies and shortcomings of social judg-
    ment. Englewood Cliffs, N.J.: Prentice-
    Hall, 1980.
Rogers, C.R. On becoming a person. Boston:
    Houghton Mifflin, 1961.
Tversky, A., and Kahneman, D. Belief in the
    law of small numbers. Psychological Bulletin,
    1971, 76, 105-110.
Tversky, A., and Kahneman, D. The framing of
    decisions and the psychology of choice.
    Science, 1981, 211, 453-458.
Walen, S., DiGiuseppe, R., and Wessler, R.L.
    A practitioner's guide to rational-emotive
    therapy. New York: Oxford, 1980.

Foreword

Watson, J.B., and Rayner, R. Conditioned emotional
    reactions. Journal of Experimental Psychology,
    1920, 3, 1-14.
Wessler, R.A., and Wessler, R.L. The principles
    and practice of rational-emotive therapy.
    San Francisco: Jossey-Bass, 1980.
Wessler, R.L. Alternative conceptions of rational-
    emotive therapy: Towards a philosophically
    neutral psychotherapy. Paper presented
    at 12th European Congress of Behavior Therapy,
    September 5, 1982, Rome, Italy.
Zajonc, R.B. Feeling and thinking: Preferences
    need no inferences. American Psychologist,
    1980, 35, 151-175.

PART ONE: FUNDAMENTALS

Chapter One

RATIONAL-EMOTIVE THERAPY: THEORETICAL PERSPECTIVES

All approaches to psychotherapy rest on a number of explicit or implicit theoretical foundations. They all posit an underlying image of the person. They all make statements concerning what constitutes psychological health and psychological disturbance, how psychological disturbance is acquired and how it is perpetuated. Finally, they all put forward viewpoints concerning how individuals change, i.e. how people can overcome their psychological problems. In this chapter, I wish to offer the rational-emotive position on these points. This statement should serve as the theoretical explanatory framework for the other chapters in the book.

1.   IMAGE OF THE PERSON

Ellis (1979a) argues that humans are basically hedonistic. Their main purposes are to stay alive and to pursue and maximise their happiness while being mindful that this is to be done within the context of a social world. In other words, while humans had primarily better be self-interested, they had better take into account the goals of others with whom they are involved. Thus, 'self-interest' is not to be equated with 'selfishness' – which means cynically disregarding the goals and purposes of others (Ellis and Becker, 1982). The individuality of humans is stressed. It is noted that humans differ markedly in what will bring them happiness. Parenthetically, it is not a primary task of rational-emotive therapists to show clients what will bring them happiness, but how they block themselves from pursuing it and how they can remove these blocks.

Rational-Emotive Therapy: Theoretical Perspectives

1.1 <u>Rationality</u>.   In RET theory, rational
does not have any fixed definition.   It means that
which aids and abets individuals in achieving their
basic goals and purposes.   While 'irrational' means
that which prevents or blocks them from reaching
these goals and purposes.

1.2 <u>Human   Fallibility</u>.   Rational-emotive
theory posits that humans are by nature fallible and
not perfectible.   They have a biological tendency to
make errors and defeat themselves in the pursuit of
their basic goals and purposes.   This roots RET in
humanistic philosophy, since humans are urged to
accept themselves for their humanity, i.e. their
fallibility.

1.3 <u>Human Complexity and Fluidity</u>.   Humans
are regarded as being enormously complex organisms.
They have innumerable traits, aspects, values,
beliefs, behaviours, etc.   Furthermore, humans are
deemed to be constantly in flux rather than static.
They have the potential to effect changes in
virtually all of their psychological processes and
are thus urged to view themselves as ever-changing
(rather than fixed) organisms.

1.4 <u>Human Activity</u>.   RET theory stresses that
human beings can best achieve their basic values and
goals by <u>actively</u> pursuing them.   They are less
likely to be successful in this regard if they are
passive or half-hearted in their pursuits.

1.5 <u>Biological   Emphasis</u>.   Ellis   (1979b)
argues that human beings have two basic tendencies
both being rooted in their biological heritage.
First, humans are deemed to have a biological
tendency towards irrationality.   They are not taught
to act irrationally in the absence of such a
tendency (Ellis, 1976).   Some of the arguments Ellis
puts forward in favour of his 'biological hypothesis' include the following:

(a)   Virtually all humans show evidence of major
      human irrationalities.
(b)   Major irrationalities are to be found in
      virtually all social and cultural groups.
(c)   Many human irrationalities actually go counter
      to the teachings of parents, peers and the mass
      media (e.g. people are not taught that it is
      good to procrastinate but countless do so).
(d)   Major human irrationalities are to be found in
      the highly intelligent, educated and gifted.
(e)   Humans who are opposed to irrationalities
      often fall prey to them.

(f)   An understanding of irrational activity does not in itself help overcome it.

(g)   Humans often adopt other irrationalities after giving up former irrationalities.

(h)   Humans often go back to irrational activity even though they have often worked hard to overcome it.

(i)   It is often very difficult for humans to overcome their irrationalities. (Ellis, 1976).

Although this may appear to be a gloomy view, humans' second basic tendency, in fact, makes the rational-emotive image of the person an optimistic one. Humans are deemed to have great potential to work to change their biologically based irrationalities and to actualize themselves and achieve greater enjoyment. The key factors here, as will be shown later, are persistent work and effort. Ellis (1979a) claims that if humans will actively and persistently work to overcome their psychological disturbances they will often, although not always, achieve a large measure of success.

1.6 The Importance of Cognition in Human Experience. Ellis (1962) has stated that emotional experience cannot be considered separately from other modes such as sensing, thinking and acting and has maintained this interactive position in subsequent years. However, he considers that the most efficient way of effecting lasting emotional and behavioural change is for people to change their thinking. Thus, cognition is given special emphasis in his theory. Various types of cognitive processes are discussed in rational-emotive theory and these are outlined in the following model of an emotional episode (originated by Wessler and Wessler, 1980).

At step 1, the person is confronted with a stimulus configuration which is deemed to exist independently of the person confronting it (much has been written on the philosophical problems implicit in this statement, but it is an assumption made in this model). At step 2, the person registers a portion of the stimulus configuration in his sensory apparatus. However, this does not have to be within the person's awareness. At step 3, the person could, potentially at least, give a purely descriptive account of what occurred at step 2 (e.g. "the man was walking in the direction of the post office carrying an envelope", as opposed to "the man was going to post a letter"). At step 4, the person makes interpretations of the data gained at steps 2 and 3. This involves going beyond the data at hand and includes such activities as guess-

---

STEP 1:   STIMULUS CONFIGURATION

STEP 2:   DETECTION

STEP 3:   DESCRIPTION

STEP 4:   INFERENCE (Descriptive-Evaluative)

STEP 5:   PERSONAL SIGNIFICANCE (Evaluative)

STEP 6:   EMOTIONAL EXPERIENCE

STEP 7:   BEHAVIOUR

STEP 8:   REINFORCING CONSEQUENCES (of steps 6 and 7)

Free-floating step: <u>DECISIONS</u>

---

ing the intentions of others' actions, making forecasts about the data at hand and assessing the implications of one's behaviours for self and others. Wessler and Wessler (1980) argue that 'step 4' cognitions are non-evaluative in nature but this is strictly speaking not universally true. Thus, the statement: "He acted badly" is an evaluative statement but one which does not yet clarify the emotional experience of the person making the statement. Step 5 cognitions are evaluative in nature and indicate the personal significance of the event for the person concerned. It is step 5 cognitions that enable us to understand the person's emotional experience at step 6. Behaviours at step 7 are deemed to follow 'personal significancies' and give rise to responses from the physical and social environment at step 8 which have reinforcement or punishment value for the individual and which in turn have a potential effect on the person's future behaviour. Decisions are free-floating in the model in that the person can decide to make changes at steps 2, 3, 4, 5, and 7 (emotions are very difficult to change directly) which have ramifications at other steps in the model.

This model is an extension of Ellis' (1962) ABC model in which 'A' refers to an activating event; 'B' - the person's belief about the event and 'C' -

the emotional and behavioural consequences of adhering to the belief. 'A' in Ellis' model comprises
steps 1-4 in Wessler and Wessler's (1980) model, 'B'
is equivalent to step 5 and 'C' refers to steps 6
and 7.

2.   CONCEPTIONS OF PSYCHOLOGICAL DISTURBANCE AND
     PSYCHOLOGICAL HEALTH

     2.1 Rational and Irrational Beliefs.   Ellis
has addressed himself mainly to two processes at
step 5 in the model just outlined. He calls these
processes: rational and irrational beliefs.   In
terms of the model, rational beliefs are matters of
personal significance which are non-absolute in
nature. They indicate desire, preference, want and
wish.   When humans get what they desire they experience emotions which indicate pleasure and when
they do not get what they want they experience
emotions which indicate displeasure, such as sadness, annoyance, concern and responsibility. These
are emotions that Ellis considers to be negative but
appropriate to negative activating events in that
they do not significantly inferfere with the pursuit
of established personal goals or, if these are for-
ever blocked, the selection and pursuit of new
goals. These 'rational'[1] emotions then stem from
rational beliefs which are non-absolute statements
of personal significance.

     Irrational beliefs are matters of personal
significance which are stated in absolute terms such
as 'must', 'should', 'ought', and 'have to'. Ellis
often writes about individuals escalating their
desires into demands. Thus, these two processes can
be linked.   Emotions which stem from adherence to
irrational beliefs include depression, anger,
anxiety and guilt - emotions that Ellis considers to
be negative and inappropriate to negative activating events. These emotions can be deemed to be
irrational in that they generally impede the pursuit
of basic goals. Even if people get what they deem
they 'must', they are not happy because of the prospect of losing it. Ellis (1982) further claims that
rational beliefs underlie functional behaviours,
while irrational beliefs underpin dysfunctional
behaviours, such as withdrawal, procrastination,
substance abuse, alcoholism, etc.

     Irrational beliefs, according to Ellis, are
absolute demands on reality (namely on self, others
and the world). They are thus anti-empirical in
that they often fly in the face of reality. For
example, if I demand: "I must get what I want", I

am implying that there exists a universal law which
leads me to get what I want, which is empirically
false.   Thus, for example, £1 million does not
appear when I want it to appear even though I demand
it do so.   The rational version: I want what I want
(but I don't have to get it) is empirically correct
on two points.   First, the belief indicates that my
desire exists and secondly it points out that there
is no law of the universe which indicates that I
will get what I want merely by wanting it.   As will
be shown in later chapters, Ellis constantly tries
to help his clients see the distinction between an
empirical law of the universe and a self-created
demand on reality.   His purpose is to show people
that what they consider to be a universal law really
exists in their minds and thus is amenable to change
(to   the   non-absolute   version).   This   method   is
called philosophical disputing.   It is paralleled by
pragmatic disputing where the therapist points out
that   the   consequences   of   adhering   to   irrational
beliefs   are   dysfunctional   emotions   such   as   depression,   anger,   etc.   and   uses   this   negatve   consequence as a lever to engage clients in the process
of attitude change.
     The   process   of   making   absolute   demands   on
reality is called 'Musturbation'.   It is paralleled
by a process called 'Awfulising'. Awfulising is the
process of making grossly exaggerated negative conclusions when one does not get what one believes one
must or when one gets what one believes one must not
get.   Ellis considers the term awful to mean "more
than 100% bad" and to reflect the belief that "it
should not be as bad as it is".   His argument is
thus: If something happens to me that is 100% bad
and I am thinking rationally about it, I will have
the following beliefs: "I really don't like this
happening.   It is really bad.   However, there is no
law that says that this really bad thing should not
happen, so I will try and change it if I can.   If I
can't change it, I will learn to live with it and
try and get as much happiness as I can even though
this has happened.   If it really appears that this
bad thing means that I will not get any chance of
happiness in the future, I may kill myself (rational
suicide)".   Here, I have acknowledged that a 100%
bad thing has occurred and will experience strong
regret, sadness, etc.   However, if I believe that
this bad thing should not occur or it should not be
as bad as it is, I will tend to evaluate it as
awful.   Thus, awfulizing is linked to musturbation.
Wessler (1982a) has argued that these two processes

are not inevitably linked. He considers that
"awfulising" is primary and musts where they exist
are conditional: "since this would be awful, it
must not occur". Ellis counters that 'awfulising'
usually depends on musturbation. If I did not
demand that this really bad thing not be as bad as
it is I could not define something as 'awful'
because I would accept that the really bad thing has
occurred and acceptance, while acknowledging my
very strong preference, 'de-awfulises' the experience. Thus, 'awfulising' usually depends on
musturbation.

2.2 <u>Self-Acceptance and Self-Damnation</u>. A
particular type of awfulising that has received
special attention in RET is self-damnation. This
implies that I am horrible for doing something that
I must not do. Self-damnation involves two
processes, (a) the process of rating my self-hood
and rating it as totally bad, and (b) the process of
"devil-ifying" myself for being totally bad. This
second process depends on a theological concept and
implies that I should rot in hell as a subhuman
(devil). If this devil-ifying process did not occur
I could theoretically regard my self-hood as totally
bad at this time but with future potential for good.
However this is unlikely because in saying I (my
'self') am no good I am using the 'is' of identify,
which means: I = badness, and since this is my
functional core this is what I shall always be since
a fundamental core cannot change. Ellis sometimes
equates global negative self-rating with self-
damnation and sometimes distinguishes the two.
Another form in which self-damnation occurs is in
the belief many people have of being 'undeserving'
of pleasure and happiness.

The alternative to global negative self-rating
and self-damnation is self-acceptance. This
implies that I cannot legitimately rate my "self":
(1) since it is too complex to be given a single
legitimate rating, (2) since I am constantly in
flux, even if I could rate everything that has
existed about me at time 'X', 'I' would have changed
at time 'X+1' - indeed the process of rating my
"self" would lead me to change! Sharkey (1981) has
argued that self-acceptance is evaluative. He says
that if you accept your "self" as being fallible
this means that you are using the term fallible to
evaluate the "self". However this seems to me to be
a descriptive evaluation at stage 4 in the model

7

previously described and not one at step 5.   Thus I
could say at step 5 "I must not be a fallible human
being".
     Ellis adopted the concept of self-acceptance
to overcome a dilemma. He once advocated that his
clients consider themselves to be 'good' because
they were alive. However some said that they could
just as well be 'bad' because they were alive. He
then suggested that clients rate their "aliveness"
and "striving for personal fulfilment" as good and
showed them how self-rating impeded this process and
was thus "irrational".   He noticed that clients
tended to rate themselves globally (either positive
or negative) after doing or not doing something.
Thus, he identified self-rating as a conditional
process: a person considered himself good if
certain conditions applied, or bad (or less good) if
other conditions applied. His solution was to make
self-acceptance unconditional: a way of viewing
their self that people could choose not only for
sound philosophical reasons but for its pragmatic
value.   Namely the stance of self-acceptance is
'rational' in that it is likely to aid and abet
people's achieving their short and long-term goals,
while conditional self-rating is irrational in that
it is likely to impede and hinder people from
achieving their short and long-term goals. As long
as I must do 'X' to consider myself 'worthy', I will
be anxious lest I fail to achieve 'X' or anxious if
I succeed lest I fail to continue to achieve 'X'.
This anxiety will presumably impede my performance
and thus block me from my goals. Wessler's (1982a)
position that musturbation is dependent on self-
downing or self-damnation is attractive.   However,
if one considers the fundamental demand not as: I
must do 'X' in order to consider myself worthy, but
"I must consider myself worthy", Ellis' position
usually incorporates Wessler's.   The rational
alternative to this belief then is: "I can accept
myself as a fallible human no matter what".
     2.3 Discomfort Tolerance and Discomfort Dis-
turbance. Demands made on the self are central to
fundamental human disturbance *1: EGO DISTURBANCE.
Fundamental human disturbance *2 is called DIS-
COMFORT DISTURBANCE and stems from the irrational
demand: "I must feel comfortable and have comfortable life conditions". This disturbance is
manifested in a number of different ways and is
central to understanding a variety of emotional disturbances such as anger, agoraphobia, procrastination, alcoholism, etc. Conclusions that

8

stem from this premise are (1) I can't stand it, and (2) it's awful. Again while Ellis places the must-urbatory form of the belief as primary, Wessler (1982a) puts the 'awfulising' conclusion as primary with the must conditional on it. Demands made on other people either implicate ego disturbance (as in 'You must like me or I'd be no good') or discomfort disturbance ('You must like me so that you will give me what I must have') and thus do not constitute a fundamental human disturbance.

The need to be comfortable usually prevents (as shall be shown later in this chapter) people from doing the persistent and often hard work that it takes to effect productive psychological change. The ability to tolerate discomfort and frustration, not for its own sake, but so that constructive psychological changes can be made is considered a primary criterion of psychological health in RET theory. It is central to the acquisition of a philosophy of long-range hedonism -the pursuit of meaningful long-term goals while tolerating the deprivation of attractive short-term goals which are self-defeating in the longer term.

2.4 <u>Positive Mental Health</u>. Ellis (1983a) takes his central concept -musturbation - and shows how this form of thinking is involved in dogmatism, devout belief (religious and secular) and religiosity, which not surprisingly he equates with much emotional disturbance. Dogmatism, devout belief and religiosity are all based on absolute views of reality and thus according to Ellis generally sabotage humans from achieving positive mental health. He advocates thoroughgoing sceptisim as the emotionally healthy alternative. Sceptisim is based on non-absolute views of reality. Thus non-absolutism is at the core of the rational-emotive view of psychological health as can be seen as Ellis (1979b) criteria of positive mental health are outlined.

(a) <u>Self-interest</u> - As mentioned earlier, emotionally healthy people primarily put themselves first without getting completely absorbed in themselves.

(b) <u>Social interest</u> - They are concerned with the welfare of others, particularly those with whom they are intimately involved and act accordingly.

(c) <u>Self-direction</u> - They take responsibility for identifying and working towards their own chosen goals. They elicit help from others where appropriate without becoming dependent on others.

(d) Tolerance - They are able to accept others with their bad behaviour although they may actively dislike such behaviour.   They fully acknowledge that others have the right to be wrong.

(e) Acceptance of ambiguity and uncertainty - They accept that humans live in a world of uncertainty and chance.   They make decisions based on probability while acknowledging that there are no guarantees.

(f) Flexibility - They are open to change and can modify plans and courses of action according to situational changes.

(g) Scientific thinking - They tend to employ the rules of logic and scientific analysis in solving problems.   They are not cold and detached as is commonly but erroneously associated with a scientific approach to living.   Indeed they experience the full range of appropriate emotions - positive and negative.

(h) Commitment - Once they set their sights on a goal, they commit themselves fully to reaching it, doing the necessary work involved but without demanding that they achieve their goal.

(i) Risk-taking - They are prepared to take calculated risks in pursuing their goals.

(j) Self-acceptance - They accept themselves as fallible, continually changing human beings, while actively trying to change those aspects of themselves that they dislike.

(k) Acceptance of reality - They do not delude themselves as to the nature of reality.   They tend to see the world as a complex mixture of good, neutral and negative aspects.

3.   ACQUISITION AND PERPETUATION OF PSYCHOLOGICAL DISTURBANCE

3.1 Acquisition of Psychological Disturbance. Rational-emotive therapy does not posit an elaborate theory concerning how psychological disturbance is acquired.   This logically follows from Ellis' (1976; 1979b) view that humans have a strong biological tendency to think and act irrationally. While Ellis is clear that humans' tendency to make absolute commands and demands on themselves, others and the world is biologically rooted, he does acknowledge that environmental factors do contribute to emotional disturbance and thus encourage humans to make their biologically based demands (Ellis, 1979a).   He argues that because humans are particularly influenceable as young children, they tend to let themselves be overinfluenced by societal teachings such as those offered by parents, peers, teachers and the mass media (Ellis, 1979b). However, the reason that environmental control continues to wield a powerful influence over most people most of the time is because of their innate gullibility.   Individual differences play a part here also.   Humans vary in their suggestibility. Thus while some humans emerge relatively unscathed emotionally from harsh and severe childhood regimes, others emerge emotionally damaged from more benign regimes (Werner and Smith, 1982). Thus, Ellis strongly believes that we, as humans, are not made disturbed by our experiences.   Rather we bring our ability to disturb ourselves to our experiences.

While past experiences do contribute but do not cause humans to make absolute demands on reality (step 5 of Wessler and Wessler's model), such experiences do tend to have a greater impact on the inferences that humans make about reality (step 4 of the model).   Thus, if a woman is exposed to many harsh critical males early on in her life, she will tend to expect that most men will be harsh and critical.   However, she will then, Ellis would argue, have the biological tendency to (a) conclude that all men are like this, and (b) needlessly upset herself about this so-called 'reality', i.e. to 'musturbate' and 'awfulize' about this 'fact'.

3.2 Perpetuation of Psychological Disturbance.   While RET does not have an elaborate theory of the acquisition of psychological disturbance, it does have a more extensive theory to explain how people perpetuate their disturbance. First, most people perpetuate their psychological disturbance precisely because of their own theories concerning the 'cause' of their problems.   They do not have what Ellis (1979b) calls "RET Insight 1": that psychological disturbance is mainly 'caused' by the beliefs that people hold about the negative events in their lives.   They tend to attribute the 'cause' of their problems to the situations themselves rather than to their beliefs about these situations.   Lacking 'insight 1', people are ignorant of the major determinants of their disturbance.   Consequently they do not know what to change to overcome their difficulties.   Even when individuals clearly see that their beliefs determine their disturbance, they may lack 'RET Insight 2': that they remain upset by re-indoctrinating themselves <u>in the present</u> with these beliefs. People who do see that their beliefs determine their disturbance tend to perpetuate such disturbance by devoting their energy to attempting to find out <u>why</u> and <u>how</u> they adopted such beliefs instead of using such energy to change the presently-held beliefs. Some people who have both insights still perpetuate their disturbance because they lack 'RET Insight 3': "Only if we constantly <u>work</u> and <u>practice</u> in the present as well as in the future to <u>think,</u> feel and act <u>against</u> these irrational beliefs are we likely to surrender them and make ourselves significantly less disturbed" (Ellis, 1979b, p. 47). Such people believe that just seeing that a belief is irrational is sufficient for change to take place.

Ellis (1979b) stresses that the major reason why people fail to change is due to their philosophy of 'low frustration tolerance' (LFT). As mentioned earlier, people who adhere to such a philosophy, tend to believe that they <u>must</u> be comfortable and that they <u>can't stand</u> to <u>feel</u> frustrated. Thus, they will <u>tend to avoid</u> the discomfort that working to effect psychological change very often involves even though facing and enduring such short-term discomfort will probably result in long-term benefit. As Wessler (1978) has noted such people are operating hedonistically from their frame of reference. They evaluate the tasks associated with change as 'too uncomfortable to bear' - certainly more painful than the psychological disturbance to which they have achieved a fair measure of habituation. They prefer to opt for the comfortable discomfort, thus perpetuating their disturbance rather than face the "change-related" discomfort which they rate as "dire". Clearly therapists have to intervene in this closed system of beliefs if psychological change is to be effected. This philosophy of low frustration tolerance which impedes change can take many different forms. For example, Maultsby (1975) notes that people avoid an activity which would be in their long-term interest to perform because of the 'neurotic fear of feeling a phony'. Such a person might say: "I didn't feel <u>me</u>" or "It didn't feel natural". Another prevalent form of LFT is 'anxiety about anxiety'. Here individuals may not expose themselves to anxiety-provoking situations because they are afraid that they might become anxious if they did so - a prospect which would be evaluated as 'terrible'.

'Anxiety about anxiety' represents an example of a phenomenon that further accounts for why people perpetuate their psychological disturbances. Ellis (1979b) has noted that people often make themselves disturbed about their disturbances. Thus they block themselves from working to overcome their original psychological disturbance because they are up-setting themselves about having the original dis-turbance. Humans are often inventive in this respect. Thus they can make themselves anxious about their anxiety, depressed about being dep-ressed, guilty concerning their anger, etc. Con-sequently, people often have to overcome their secondary disturbances before embarking on effecting change in their original problems.

Ellis (1979b) has observed that people some-times experience some kind of perceived payoff for their psychological disturbance other than gaining immediate obvious ease. Here such disturbance may be perpetuated until the perceived payoff is dealt with to minimise its impact. For example, a woman who claims to want to lose weight may not take the necessary steps because she fears that losing weight would make her more attractive to men, a situation which she would view as 'dire'. Thus, remaining fat protects her (in her mind) from a 'terrible' state of affairs. It is to be stressed that rational-emotive theorists stress the phenomenological nature of these payoffs, i.e. it is the person's view of the 'payoff' that is important in deter-mining its impact not the event delineated in the person's description. In a similar vein Tschudi (1977), a personal construct theorist, has noted that people often do not move towards their stated or desired goals because such goals have negative implications. Thus a man may not work towards giving up his anger because he believes that in doing so he will become less sensitive. Rational-emotive therapists would not only search for in-ferential errors (step 4 cognitions) in such cases but also look for the implicit irrational beliefs (step 5 cognitions) which are often involved, e.g. "If I become less sensitive I would be less worthy'.

Another way people tend to perpetuate their psychological disturbance is explained by the 'self-fulfilling prophecy' phenomenon (Jones, 1977; Wachtel, 1977). People tend to become fixed in their expectations for their own and other people's behaviour. In doing so they tend to act according to their own predictions (e.g. I'll stammer when I speak on the telephone) or they tend to elicit actions from others which serve as confirmatory evidence for their original hypotheses (e.g. assuming others will be unfriendly —— acting unfriendly —— which elicits an unfriendly reaction from others). Here, as Wachtel (1977) has shown, people are often deprived of new information which might make a difference to their internal constructions. It is important to note that self-fulfilling prophecies mainly lead to the perpetuation of inferential errors (step 4) which in turn serve as cues for the person making absolute demands on reality (step 5). If the inferential errors were corrected the person would not have the cue for making such demands. This may not mean that the person has made evaluative changes at step 5 since the trigger has been removed[2].

4.   THEORY OF PSYCHOLOGICAL CHANGE

Rational-emotive therapists are quite ambitious in setting as their major therapeutic goal helping clients to effect what Ellis often calls a 'profound philosophic change'. This primarily involves their clients surrendering their 'demanding' philosophy and replacing it with a 'desiring' philosophy. Not all clients can achieve such a personal revolution (Mahoney, 1980) and thus therapists sometimes settle with some clients for effecting inferential and/or behavioural changes.

In achieving such philosophical restructuring individuals tend to do the following:
(1) They adhere to the idea that they manufacture and keep on manufacturing their own psychological disturbance.
(2) They fully acknowledge that they have the ability to change such disturbances to a significant degree.
(3) They understand that their psychological disturbance is mainly determined by irrational beliefs. Furthermore they know how to identify such beliefs when they become disturbed.
(4) They know how to dispute such beliefs cognitively using logicoempirical scientific methods and to replace these with their rational alternatives.
(5) They then proceed to reinforce such cognitive learning by working persistently hard in employing emotive and behavioural methods.

They tolerate the discomfort that doing this may well involve but they recognize that without acting on newly acquired learnings, change will probably not be maintained.

(6) They acknowledge that as humans they will probably have difficulty in effecting a profound philosophic change and will tend as a result to backslide. Taking such factors into account they re-employ and continually practice the multimodal methods that RET advocates for the rest of their lives. In doing so they learn to experiment and find the methods that work especially well for them[3]. They specifically recognise that forceful and dramatic methods are powerful ways of aiding philosophic change and readily implement these particularly at times when they experience difficulty in changing (Ellis, 1979c).

NOTES

1. Ellis does not often refer to emotions as being rational or irrational but since they are experiences that either enhance or inhibit striving for goals, they can be considered in this way; he refers to them rather as "functional" or "dysfunctional". It is difficult to see the difference between dysfunctional and irrational.

2. The focus in this section has been mainly on the perpetuation of psychological disturbance determined by a person's continued belief in various irrationalities. As noted above, such perpetuation is further contributed to by the person continuing to make inferential distortions. Beck et al. (1979) and Burns (1980) have discussed at length how such thinking errors are perpetuated. These sources should be consulted as the topic remains outside of the scope of this chapter.

3. I have restricted the discussion in this section to philosophic change. As noted earlier, when such change is not forthcoming rational-emotive therapists aim to effect inferential and behavioural change. In these cases, their theory of such psychological change would not necessarily differ from other cognitive-behavioural therapists.

Chapter Two

THE EFFECTIVE PRACTICE OF RATIONAL-EMOTIVE THERAPY[1]

Effective psychotherapy, of whatever orientation, occurs when the therapist both correctly
applies appropriate therapeutic methods and
successfully manages the inter-personal aspects of
the therapeutic relationship.   When this is
achieved, both participants in the therapeutic
enterprise and any independent observer have the
clear sense that here is a team working together in
a collaborative fashion towards goals identified by
the client. The purpose of this paper is twofold:
(1) to demonstrate how rational-emotive therapists
develop an effective working alliance with their
clients, and (2) to outline the major therapeutic
techniques of Rational-Emotive Therapy (RET).

1.   DEVELOPING AN EFFECTIVE THERAPEUTIC ALLIANCE
IN RET

Here, the conceptual work of Bordin (1975,
1976) will be employed. Bordin's theoretical work
has done much to elevate the concept of the therapeutic alliance to a position of greater conceptual
clarity. Bordin (1976) refers to the term "working
alliance" by which he means:
     ". . . the complex of understandings and
     attachments that are formed when a person in a
     state of personal crisis . . . turns to
     another for his or her expert help and a
     contract is made. This contract or alliance is
     a subtle mixture of explicit and implicit un-
     derstandings and acknowledged and un-
     acknowledged attachments" (p.2.).
In clarifying this complexity, Bordin (1975)
cites the goals, tasks, and bonds which make up the
working alliance.   The goals are the 'ends' of the
therapeutic journey, the tasks are the 'means' for

achieving such ends, while the bonds refer to the quality of the relationship of the two travellers. Disruption to the journey might occur because the travellers do not get on (weak bonding), disagree on journey's end (non-agreement on goals), and/or because they prefer different ways of reaching their destination (non-agreement on tasks).

1.1 <u>Effective bonds</u>. The effective bonds that rational-emotive therapists seek to develop with clients are collaborative in nature, with the rational part of the client allied with the therapist against the irrational part of the client. The irrational part of the client is considered to be that part of the client which prevents him from achieving his long-term self-enhancing goals. The therapist (1) offers the client unconditional acceptance of the latter as a fallible human being, (2) is empathic and genuine in the therapeutic encounter, (3) is not unduly warm towards the client becaue this is considered to be counter-therapeutic from a long-term perspective, in that the client's approval and dependency needs may be reinforced.

It is important to underline that there is no one way of developing effective bonds with clients. What is important is for the therapist to convey to the client that she is a trustworthy and know-ledgeable individual who is prepared to totally commit herself to the task of helping the client reach his goals. It is important that the therapist develop the kind of relationship with the client that the latter will, according to his idiosyncratic position, find helpful. This might mean that, with some clients, the therapist might emphasise her expertness and portray herself as a well-qualified individual whose knowledge and expertise form the basis of what social psychologists call <u>com-municator credibility</u>. Such credibility is im-portant to the extent that certain clients will more likely listen to the therapist if she stresses these characteristics. Other clients, however, will be more likely to listen to the therapist if the latter portrays herself as a likeable individual. Such a therapist might de-emphasise her expertness, but emphasise her humanity by being prepared to disclose certain aspects of her life which are both relevant to the client's own problems and which emphasise liking as a powerful source of communicator credibility.

For example, I recently saw two clients on the same day with whom I emphasised different aspects of communicator credibility. I decided to interact with Jim, a 30 year-old bricklayer, in a casual, laid-back style. I encouraged him to use my first name and was prepared to disclose some personal details because I believed from what he had told me in an assessment interview, that he strongly disliked "stuffy mind doctors who treat me as another case rather than a human being". However, in the next hour with Jane, a 42 year-old unmarried fashion editor, I portrayed myself as "Dr Dryden" and emphasised my long training and qualifications because she indicated, again in an assessment interview, that she would strongly dislike therapists who were too friendly and warm towards her. She wanted a therapist who "knew what he was doing". The point here is that the therapist had better be flexible with regard to changing her style of interaction with different clients. She had better come to a therapeutic decision about what style of interaction is going to be helpful in both the short- and long-term with a particular client. Furthermore the therapist needs to recognise that the style of interaction that she adopts may in fact be counter-productive (Beutler, 1979). For example, therapists had better be wary of adopting an overly friendly style of interaction with "hysterical" clients. No matter what style of interaction the therapist adopts with a particular client, it is important for the therapist to be concerned, genuine and empathic in the encounter.

1.2 <u>Agreement on goals</u>. It is extremely important that client and therapist share a common understanding concerning the client's goals. By goals, I mean what the client hopes to achieve from therapy. This understanding is maximized when the therapist helps the client develop a PROBLEM LIST early in therapy. Here the client lists those area in his life that he regards as being problematic and that he would like to change. Items can be added to or subtracted from the problem list during the course of therapy. An additional and important aspect of the problem list concerns the client setting objectives, specifying what he would adopt as desirable outcomes in each problem area. These desired outcomes had better be stated as specifically as possible, preferably in positive terms, e.g. "I would like to feel sad rather than depressed" and "act assertively rather than withdraw in situation X". Some rational-emotive therapists think it important to develop appropriate goals for each session as well as for the entire course of therapy. This is often an effective procedure

18

although some clients in my experience may become resistant if the therapist is too compulsive about searching for goals in each particular session.

One major obstacle to the collaborative agreement on goals lies in the area of the client's desires for changes in external circumstances and/or changes in other people. While the therapist may want to agree that such goals may be possible in that the client might work toward changing the external circumstances and other people, it is important that the therapist and client both understand that primary changes are to be effected in the way the client feels, thinks and acts. An important strategy for the therapist to adopt here is to suggest to the client that they assume for the moment that the external circumstances or other people are not changeable and to discuss the various options that the client has, given this assumption. Care needs to be exercised at this point since the client may become discouraged if he thinks the therapist is saying that there is nothing that the client can do to effect the changes in external circumstances and other people that the client desires. In addition it is very difficult for the client to effect internal changes when his external situation is extremely stressful. The therapist needs to be aware of the existence of other helping agencies that may assist the client in modifying his stressful environment (e.g., social worker). Such a referral, if providing appropriate help in ameliorating the external stress, may in fact assist the client to return to therapy better equipped to effect internal changes.

1.3 Agreement on tasks. Both therapist and client have their own tasks in the therapeutic endeavour and effective therapy depends on the shared agreement on these tasks. The rational-emotive therapist's major tasks are to help the client see that (1) emotional problems have cognitive antecedents, (2) that changes in belief systems will promote both emotional and behavioural well-being and (3) that he had better continually work at changing his beliefs by employing cognitive, imaginal and behavioural methods. The client's major tasks are (1) to observe his emotional and behavioural disturbances, (2) to relate these to their cognitive determinants and (3) to continually work at changing dysfunctional beliefs by employing cognitive, imaginal and behavioural methods. Therapist and client also need to agree on the therapist's role in the process which is primarily, in RET, an active-directive one, although the therapist may become less active and directive if adopting such a stance is counter-productive to the client's style of defense. The therapist may adopt a less challenging style if the client's autonomy is easily threatened by such an interactional style. However, if the therapist is successful at communicating unconditional acceptance of the client and the latter perceives this, then the client is more likely to accept the therapist's active-directive stance.

The therapist had better be flexible in modifying her own task behaviour when this is appropriate. Thus, for example, some clients will do better in long-term RET if they are able first to relate to the therapist without interruption the historical determinants of their problems. In this case the therapist's early attempts at structuring the therapeutic process might be unproductive. One of the therapist's initial objectives in the task realm is to help structure the clients' expectations and correct any misconceptions that the client may have concerning the therapeutic endeavour and the tasks of both participants. If it is apparent that the client's expectations are at extreme variance with the tasks of the rational-emotive therapist and are resistant to structuring attempts, then the client may be better served if he is referred to a therapist who may very likely meet the client's expectations.

The therapist, however, has a number of other sub-tasks to carry out while developing and maintaining an effective therapeutic alliance with the client. Thus, the therapist had better use language that the client understands. She had better frequently check with the client that he understands what she is saying and also gauge client's reactions to her messages. This is particularly important in RET which is based on an educational model of therapy. It is also wise for the therapist to fully explain the rationale for any interventions that she intends carrying out in order to elicit the client's collaboration. Finally, as Beck et al. (1979) have pointed out, it is wise for the therapist to elicit the client's feelings and reactions to every session, being particularly sensitive to any negative reactions on the part of the client. Also a periodic review of the client's reactions to the therapeutic process is a wise procedure to initiate, since this gives both parties the opportunity to review progress and re-negotiate future goals.

It is argued here, in summary, that the techniques that rational-emotive therapists employ are likely to be more effective when both therapist and client have developed a collaborative well-bonded relationship, when they agree on the goals of the therapeutic endeavour, and when they can agree on each person's contributions to the achievement of such goals. We are now in a position to consider the major therapeutic techniques that RET therapists employ to effect therapeutic change.

2. TECHNIQUES OF EFFECTIVE RET

The aim of this section is to outline the major therapeutic changes that rational-emotive therapists employ in three areas: (1) assessment of client problems, (2) change strategies, and (3) assessment of progress.

2.1 Assessment of Client Problems. Before initiating change tactics, it is essential that the therapist undertakes an assessment of the client's major problems. While some rational-emotive therapists prefer to elicit one problem, do a thorough analysis of this problem in terms of the ABC framework, and then initiate change tactics, other therapists prefer to do a thorough assessment of all the client's major problems as outlined on the problem list in order to discern an overall picture of the client's belief system. Whatever approach the therapist favours she keeps the ABC framework very much in mind while assessing client problems.

In the ABC framework (Ellis, 1962), A stands for the client's report of the activating events; this includes inferences or non-evaluative cognitions that the client has of the event. B stands for the beliefs or evaluations that the client makes about perceived activating events. C encompasses the client's emotional and behavioural consequences which result from his evaluation at B. Rational-emotive therapists in general prefer to assess A and C before proceeding to assess the client's evaluations at B. Whether the therapist chooses to assess A or C depends both on her preferred method of working and on whether the client begins by referring to activating events or emotional and behavioural consequences.

Let us start with the situation where a client brings up an emotional or behavioural issue first. Clients often spontaneously report their emotional and/or behavioural responses to a given situation.

21

However when this spontaneous report is not forth-coming, the therapist can then adopt a number of methods to elicit the client's C. At this stage, the rational-emotive therapist can draw freely on methods originating from other major therapeutic schools but with the purpose of eliciting C (Dryden, 1982a). For example, the therapist might employ a guided imagery procedure or a gestalt exercise such as the two chair dialogue with the explicit purpose of helping the client to identify what emotions he experienced in a given situation and what actions he enacted in that situation. Once the therapist has helped the client to identify the central Cs in the episode, the therapist then procedes to assess what activating events led to the response at C.

When the therapist assesses the client's report of the activating event, she frequently employs a method called INFERENCE CHAINING (Wessler and Wessler, 1980). This method is based on the observation that clients not only make inferences concerning actual events but that these inferences are linked to further inferences in an associative stream of cognitions. Often the core inference is embedded in this stream. As an example of inference chaining, consider a situation where a client reported feeling angry. On further exploration the therapist elicited, in her assessment of A, that the client became angry in response to his boss' failure to give him due credit for a work proposal. The therapist might say: "So you were angry when your boss didn't give you due credit, is that right?" and then he might add "and the fact that he didn't give you due credit at the meeting meant what to you?". The client might reply: "Well it meant that he didn't think very much about my proposal". The therapist then enquires what is so important about having his ideas approved by his boss assuming the client inferences are true. "Well", the client my reply, "that would mean that he doesn't like me".

If no further inferences are forthcoming, the therapist then knows that she is dealing with a non-evaluative conclusion of the actual event which is expressed in the statement "My boss doesn't like me because he didn't give me due credit at the meeting". Often, while the therapist is undertaking an inference chaining assessment of a client's problem, she helps the client to identify other feelings that might underlie the originally stated feelings, in this case: anger. In the example presented the emotion was: "hurt". Once the therapist has helped the client identify the most important (embedded) inference in the inference chain and has identified correctly the emotional and behavioural consequences in the episode, she is now in a position to procede to assess the client's evaluations at point B in the ABC framework.

Before proceeding to an assessment of the client's evaluative cognitions of the inferred event, the therapist has the option of explaining the nature of evaluations and the distinction between rational and irrational evaluations. Such an explanation would deal with the issue that rational beliefs are couched in relative terms which express the client's preferences, wishes or desires about a situation, while irrational evaluations are couched in absolute terms such as demands, musts, shoulds, oughts and have to's.

In assessing the client's evaluations, the therapist will often find that the client will give additional non-evaluative cognitions or rational beliefs where she is certain, given adequate assessment of C, that the client was in fact making irrational evaluations (at B) of the event. The therapist deals with this situation by showing the client that making such rational evaluations would not, on theoretical grounds, account for the feeling that the client originally expressed. The therapist would then question the client further to determine the nature of these irrational beliefs.

In assessing irrational beliefs, the therapist adheres to an implicit model that such beliefs can be held about the self, other people, or the world or life conditions in general. These irrational beliefs may take the form of a premise which would include an absolute statement about reality e.g. a must, should or ought. Alternatively the irrational beliefs may be stated in the form of a conclusion in a situation where the inferred event violates that absolute value. Thus, if a client feels depressed about not achieving a certain grade in an examination, the therapist may be more successful at eliciting the conclusion that: "it is awful and I am no good for failing to achieve a good grade", than eliciting the irrational belief in premise form, e.g. I must achieve a good grade. Irrational evaluations stated in the form of a conclusion involve such statements as "It's awful", "I can't stand it", or "I, you, or the world in general is no good" (Ellis, 1977a).

After fully assessing the client's 'emotional episode' in terms of the ABC framework, the therapist is in a position to determine the client's goals before proceeding to the change stage of therapy. Goal assessment is important in that effective RET is carried out when both parties share a common understanding concerning the client's realistic future objectives. As mentioned above, the therapist, in assessing the client's goals, had better be aware of the client's tendency to select goals which involve changes in situations or other people, and had better help the client see that while changes may be possible, they are more likely to be made when the client is not emotionally disturbing himself about the situation. Thus, the therapist negotiates with the client to help the latter set goals which involve changes in his own emotional and/or behavioural consequences at C.

Before proceding to a description of the major change techniques involved in RET, one important aspect of assessment needs to be underscored. Quite often clients have emotional problems about their emotional and behavioural problems and a thorough-going assessment of a client's concerns had better include this secondary stage. Thus, for example, the client who reported feeling angry about his boss also, as a result of the therapist's further enquiry, reported that he felt ashamed of the fact that he was angry and hurt. One of the major reasons why it is so important for the therapist to assess problems about problems is that failure to do so would interfere with the therapist's strategies directed towards the original emotional problems. Thus if a client is ashamed of his angry feelings and the therapist merely focuses on his anger, his irrational beliefs underlying such anger may not be modified since his attention is divided between focussing on his feelings of shame about anger and working with the therapist on the irrational evaluations underlying the anger.

2.2 Change procedures. The major purpose of all change procedures is to effect changes in the client's irrational belief system. There are two ways of conceptualising the change procedures that are employed in rational-emotive therapy. First it is possible to classify procedures according to the modality employed. Here we shall look at the three major modalities used in RET. (1) Cognitive (verbal and imaginal); (2) Emotive, and (3) Behavioural. Secondly, it is possible to consider the procedures employed as to whether the therapist or client has the major responsibility for initiating the procedure.

24

2.2.1 Procedures that the Therapist is Responsible for Initiating

2.2.1.1 Cognitive methods.

One of the more commonly used procedures employed by rational emotive therapists is that of DISPUTING. Ellis (1977a) considers that there are three sub-categories of the disputing process which the therapist employs in helping clients give up irrational beliefs. These are debating, discriminating and defining.

DEBATING consists of the therapist asking the client a number of questions which are designed to help the client give up irrational beliefs. Questions such as: "What evidence supports this belief?", "In what way does it have truth or falseness?", and "What makes it so?" are frequently employed. The therapist proceeds with such questioning until the client acknowledges the falseness of his irrational belief and in addition acknowledges the truth of its rational alternative. DISCRIMINATING involves the therapist helping the client to clearly distinguish between his nonabsolute values (his wants, preferences, likes and desires) and his absolutistic values (his needs, demands and imperatives). DEFINING involves the therapist helping the client make increasingly accurate definitions in the language that he employs.

These three categories of the disputing process can be employed by the therapist to help the client make more accurate inferences about actual events (Beck et al., 1979) in addition to helping him change his irrational evaluations. Ideally, the disputing process is initiated by the therapist in the context of a socratic dialogue with the client. This involves the therapist asking the client open-ended questions and involving the client in the process so that the client is encouraged to think in a concerted manner about the irrational evaluations and inaccurate inferences that he has made. While the socratic dialogue is favoured by rational-emotive therapists, such a method is not effective with all clients. When the socratic method breaks down the therapist may introduce more explanations and not simply rely on evocative methods of disputing. One of the major purposes that the therapist has while conducting the disputing process is to help the client analyse the validity of his irrational evaluations and inaccurate inferences by helping him systematically collect evidence which demonstrates the falseness of these ideas. The therapist employs inductive questioning (Beck et al., 1979) to help the client consider alternative ways of interpreting events and appraising such events.

Particularly when helping the client dispute inaccurate inferences about events, the therapist may draw heavily on the work of Beck et al. (1979) who in their pioneering work on Cognitive Therapy have developed a number of methods to help the client re-evaluate inacurate inferences. Basically these methods involve the therapist helping the client to see what class of cognitive distortion (faulty information processing style) he is employing, and to substitute a more accurate form of information processing in its place. For example, a client may indicate that he is making a firm con-clusion when the data at his disposal does not warrant such a conclusion. The therapist might teach the client the differences between hypotheses and facts and show him he is making an arbitrary inference. She would then encourage the client to list alternative conclusions and to weigh such alternatives against the original in terms of infer-ential accuracy.

During the disputing process and at other times the therapist may employ another major cognitive technique, that of INFORMATION-GIVING. This is employed when the client reveals ignorance about some phenomenon which contributes to an inaccurate inference or irrational evaluation. For example, a common cognitive distortion that clients make is to infer that feelings of anxiety indicate that they are going crazy. The therapist may correct the client's misconception here by providing him with information about the effects of extreme anxiety. Since a large number of clients seen in mental health clinics suffer from such a misconception - termed phrenophobia by Raimy (1975) -providing such information often serves to correct such a mis-conception.

Another major cognitive technique that the therapist employs is that of INTERPRETATION OF DEFENSES. It is well known that clients are likely to either deny the existence of an emotional problem or distort the extent that the emotional problem exists. When the therapist suspects such defensive behaviour on the part of the client he tests out such a hypothesis by searching for hidden self-condemnation which serves as a motivating force for the client employing such defensive strategies. By helping the client to accept himself for his emotional problem, rational-emotive therapists are often able to help the client to fully admit to the existence of such problems.

While the above cognitive methods are primarily verbal, rational-emotive therapists also employ IMAGERY methods. A common imagery method that is used in the course of disputing irrational beliefs and inaccurate inferences is that of time projection. The purpose of time projection is to help the client move beyond immediate inter-pretations and evaluations and thereby to view events from an increasingly greater time perspective. This is often employed as an indirect disputing method. The client is helped to see, as the therapist projects further into the future, that events judged as "awful" at the present time are evaluated in a less extreme manner when viewed from a different time perspective. Thus, for example, I often employ time projection techniques with students who evaluate an examination failure as a 'dreadful', 'horrible' experience. By helping them move forward in time from the presumed failure, the client is able to see that although failure is a bad experience, it is not the 'end of the world' experience that it seems to be at the present time.

Another imagery method that is sometimes employed, although perhaps not favoured, by rational-emotive therapists is HYPNOSIS. Rational-emotive therapists tend to employ hypnosis when the client seems to favour such a method. A hypnotic paradigm is employed in which the more traditional forms of disputing are employed (Reardon, Tosi and Gwynne, 1977).

2.2.1.2 Emotive methods. Critics of RET often make the point that it is lacking in its emphasis on the emotive modality. This is in fact a misconception since rational-emotive therapists often employ such methods. One major emotive method that the therapist employs is: UNCONDITIONAL ACCEPTANCE of the client. The therapist's purpose here is to demonstrate that no matter how obnoxious the client's behaviour is, not only to the therapist but to other people in the client's life, she accepts the client as a fallible human being, who can and often does act badly. Unconditional acceptance of the client is not only often com-municated by the therapist's attitude and her behaviour towards the client, but can also be communicated by the frank disclosure of the therapist's position to the client. Unconditional acceptance does not mean that the therapist accepts everything about the client. The point is that while the therapist may not condone or even like certain client behaviours, she can accept the client as a human being who acts in undesirable ways.

Another important therapist initiated emotive method is that of <u>therapist</u> SELF-DISCLOSURE. The rational-emotive therapist is not shy to admit her own failings and fallibilities, but in doing so shows that she can fully accept herself for such aspects. She can frankly admit that she may not like aspects of herself but refuses to damn herself for these unlikable aspects. In doing so the therapist often serves as a role model for the client in the teaching of rational principles.

The rational-emotive therapist often employs HUMOUR in therapy sessions. Such humour is directed either at aspects of the client (never at the client himself) or at aspects of the therapist's own behaviour (but never at the therapist herself). The aim of the therapist here is to help the client adopt a stance of "not taking oneself and one's problems too seriously", and is often an effective way of loosening up a client in therapy. Another humorous method often employed particularly by Ellis (1977b) is that of HUMOROUS SONGS which often communicate a rational principle. This method is often employed in groups but can also be employed in individual therapy. There is indeed a tape of rational humorous songs which clients may be encouraged to listen to and perhaps to sing at various times to aid the process of self-disputing (Ellis, 1977b).

Rational-emotive therapists often employ ANALOGIES and PARABLES in their teaching of rational principles. Thus, for example, the case of Nathan Leopold[2] is often related to clients who condemn themselves as thoroughly rotten individuals for committing some presumed sin. The purpose here is to help the client see that doing something seriously wrong does not make him a bad person and that by accepting himself he is less likely in the future to act badly.

Rational-emotive therapists often employ other emotive-dramatic methods in therapy to teach rational concepts and/or aid them in the disputing process. The therapist is only limited by her own imagination when it comes to devising such methods. However, it is important for the therapist to monitor the effects of such dramatic techniques, preferably by asking the client at the end of the session his reaction to such methods. Perhaps such methods had better not be employed with clients who have enduring negative reactions to them. The dramatic methods that rational-emotive therapists employ aim to encourage the client to raise his level of frustration tolerance and to accept himself as a fallible human. Thus, the therapist might, in the course of talking to the client about self-acceptance for acting foolishly, suddenly leap to the floor and start barking like a dog. The startled client is then asked for his reaction towards the therapist for such behaviour. Is the client going to condemn the therapist for acting in such a foolish way in the same way that he might condemn himself? Often such dramatic methods serve to reinforce the message that is communicated in the more traditional verbal disputing process.

Another emotive method that the therapist may initiate in the change process is ROLE-PLAYING - to either aid the client in behaviour rehearsal or to aid the disputing process (rational role reversal). In RATIONAL ROLE REVERSAL the therapist may speak for the irrational part of the client and encourage the client to take the role of the rational part of himself. The purpose here is to help the client improve his skill at answering back and responding to his irrational voice. This is best done with clients who show some prior skill at self-disputing.

2.2.1.3 Behavioural methods. While most of the behavioural methods employed in rational-emotive therapy are the responsibility of the client to initiate, the rational-emotive therapist can initiate a number of SKILL-TRAINING methods to, for example, improve a client's social skills, to help the client develop skills at self-assertion, or to help a client become a more proficient problem-solver. While such skills are not specifically designed to help clients change their inferences or beliefs about events, they often have that secondary effect. Thus the client who is able to assert himself with his boss may learn in the process that nothing awful will happen as a result of such assertion. However, rational-emotive therapists generally employ such skills training while reminding clients that negative responses from others, or negative outcomes in the environment may very well follow, and in so doing initiate the disputing of any inaccurate inferences or ir-rational evaluations that the client might make con-cerning such responses and outcomes.

2.2.2 <u>Procedures</u> that the Client is Responsible for Initiating

The techniques that clients are responsible for initiating are all designed to help them put into practice in their everyday life what they have learned during therapy sessions. The purpose here is to help the client become autonomous from the therapist and in a sense become his own therapist. The therapist has an important role to play in helping the client initiate such techniques outside the session. Thus the therapist had better fully explain the rationale of any techniques that he suggests the client use outside therapy. She had better teach the technique to the client in a very clear and concise fashion and get feedback that the client understands and accepts the validity and purpose of the procedure. Furthermore the therapist must in advance determine any obstacles that the client might anticipate experiencing which might prevent him from carrying out the procedure. In addition, the therapist had better make it a priority to follow up and discuss with the client his experiences in executing the procedure, or if the client did not carry out the procedure to determine the reasons which prevented him from doing so. However, since the therapist cannot make the client carry out an effective technique outside of the session, the client's major responsibility is initiating such techniques for himself.

2.2.2.1 <u>Cognitive methods</u>.

The client can and indeed had better employ for himself the same disputing techniques that the therapist employs with him in the session. Thus, for example, the client can use several HOMEWORK FORMS that are available for the purpose of debating. The client takes a disturbing emotion or self-defeating action, writes down the context in which this occurred and using the instruction - 'cherchez le should' (look for the should) - determines for himself what (if any) irrational evaluations he was making in the situation. He can then move on to debate the truth or falseness of such beliefs and if they are found to be false replace them with rational beliefs. The more that a client learns to dispute his irrational beliefs the more likely he is to believe in the rational alternative. Another technique that the client can get out of the session which has been designed to help him dispute his irrational beliefs is a technique called <u>DIBS</u> (Disputing irrational beliefs, Ellis, 1977c). The client is provided with a structure in which he can

ask himself six questions and his task is to come up with as many answers to each question as he can:
(1)   What irrational beliefs do I want to dispute and surrender?
(2)   Can I rationally support this belief?
(3)   What evidence exists of the truth of this belief?
(4)   What evidence exists of the falseness of my belief that I must . . . ?
(5)   What are the worst possible things that could actually happen to me if I . . . ?
(6)   What good things could happen or could I make happen if I never . . . ?

The client, of course, fills in the blanks with the content of his particular irrational belief.

Client-initiated DISCRIMINATING involves first the detection of an irrational belief, then writing the rational alternative to this belief and clearly providing reasons why they are different and what different effects each type of belief would have. He might also provide himself with reasons why he would prefer to adopt the rational belief as opposed to the irrational belief. In addition, other aspects of discrimination include the client showing himself adaptive as well as maladaptive aspects of his behaviour, observing the distinction between undesirable and 'unbearable' results in his life, clearly showing to himself that hassles to not equal 'horrors' and clearly distinguishing between logical conclusions about his life and those which do not follow.

Using DEFINING techniques, the client learns to write down both his evaluations and his inferences and in doing so learns to identify and correct the semantic errors in his thinking. Thus, for example, a client might search for over-generalisations in his thinking, particularly those which are associated with the verb 'to be'. Thus, when a client writes 'I am a fool', he might correct himself by reminding himself that if that were true he would only be able to act foolishly and might correct his semantic error by saying 'I am a person who acted foolishly in this instance'. The above three methods of debating, discriminating and defining clearly rest on the client's ability to detect and to record his thoughts, inferences and beliefs. Thus the therapist had better help the client whenever the client shows difficulty in the detection process.

While the self-disputing techniques are of great importance in RET, there are other cognitive techniques that the client can initiate to reinforce learnings derived from therapy sessions. Thus, for example, he can initiate BIBLIOTHERAPY. This involves the therapist suggesting certain self-help books or novels with a particular therapeutic purpose for the client to read outside the session. While the therapist had better make sure that the reading material he is suggesting is suitable for the client's reading level and comprehension level, the client had better negotiate with the therapist an appropriate amount of material to read. After the material has been read it is best for the client to discuss with the therapist what he has learnt from the material.

Two cognitive techniques which are designed to help the client practice his new rational philosophy are (1) EMPLOYING NEW RATIONAL SELF-STATEMENTS IN A WRITTEN FORM, and (2) USING RET WITH OTHERS. In the first technique the client takes a 3" x 5" white card and writes on it a new rational self-statement which he then carries around, looks at and repeats a number of times daily, particularly at times when he is vulnerable to emotional distress. Such a card serves as a helpful therapeutic aide-memoire in a situation where the client might not make a spontaneous rational response to his irrational evaluation. Using RET with others provides the client with an opportunity to rehearse rational messages for himself. It also provides him with an opportunity to think through rational arguments, for he is likely to meet opposition when he comes to debate such ideas as: 'It is not necessary to gain the approval of a significant other'. If the client is prepared for such opposition and is discouraged from believing that he must convince the other person of the correctness of his own position, then such a proselytizing technique has much potential value, particularly if the other person is willing to constructively debate the issue at hand with the client.

Two further cognitive techniques that the client can employ involves him learning to cope with heightened emotional reactions and help him resist self-defeating behavioural responses. These are self-instructional training and distraction techniques. SELF-INSTRUCTIONAL TRAINING was originated by Meichenbaum (1977) and involves the client talking to himself in constructive ways in order to cope with extreme emotional reactions. Thus, for example, a client who becomes very anxious may initiate such rational self-talk as 'this is only anxiety, it is not dangerous, it is merely uncomfortable and I can cope with it'. In addition, self-instructional training may be used to overcome avoidance prior to entering a threatening situation. Here the client can instruct himself to keep his emotional reaction within manageable bounds.

DISTRACTION METHODS serve a similar purpose in controlling the client's emotional reaction but involve the client redirecting his attention away from his emotional experiences to specific aspects in his environment. Thus, a client who is particularly anxious in a given situation might re-focus his attention and describe to himself in great detail an object that is present in the anxiety-provoking environment. In addition the client might distract himself from his own emotional reactions by instructing himself to initiate a relaxation procedure and then to carry out the procedure in a given situation.

The client can also employ several IMAGERY techniques for himself outside of the session. Thus for example, the client can carry out procedures suggested by Arnold Lazarus (1978). Two imagery techniques that rational-emotive therapists encourage clients to initiate for themselves outside of the session mainly are: rational-emotive imagery and cognitive (imagery) rehearsal. RATIONAL-EMOTIVE IMAGERY was designed to help the client bridge the gap between intellectual and emotional insight. The purpose of the technique is to provide the client with practice at holding a new rational belief and/or getting practice at changing his emotional experience from a dysfunctional to a functional one.

There are two forms of rational-emotive imagery, one devised by Maultsby and one modified by Ellis (Maultsby and Ellis, 1974). In the Maultsby version of rational-emotive imagery, the client is encouraged to visualise the activating event which is often the worst that the client can realistically imagine. Whilst keeping such an image clearly in his mind the client is encouraged to practice the new rational belief that had previously been identified by the process of disputing. The client is encouraged to go over the rational belief in his mind's eye and is then asked to observe changes in his emotional reactions. The client is then encouraged to practice this procedure several times a day usually over a 30-day period.

In the Ellis version of rational-emotive imagery, the client is again encouraged to imagine the activating event and is further encouraged to experience the same dysfunctional emotions that he would normally experience when exposed to such an event. He is then encouraged to change such a negative dysfunctional feeling to a negative functional feeling (for example, changing from depression to sadness, from anger to annoyance, from anxiety to concern). The client is asked to signal to the therapist when he is able to do this and then the therapist asks the client how he managed to change his feelings from a dysfunctional to a functional one. The client invariably says that he achieved such a change by changing his beliefs about the activating event. The client is then encouraged to carry out this procedure on his own several times a day, again for a 30-day period.

In COGNITIVE REHEARSAL the client prepares himself, for example, to enter an avoided situation and mentally rehearses approaching that particular situation while repeating to himself such rational self-statements that have been developed during the disputing process. Raimy (1975) has written that it is the repeated review of such events in imagery that is important. Thus the client is encouraged to repeatedly rehearse such new cognitive and behavioural responses before actually doing this in real life. This procedure is particularly valuable for clients who claim that they cannot 'see' themselves putting into practice these new responses (Lazarus, 1978).

2.2.2.2 Emotive methods. The emotive techniques that a client can initiate for himself often involve a dramatic forceful and vigorous quality (Ellis, 1979c). For example, the client may be encouraged to rehearse rational self-statements in a passionate and vigorous manner, where he adopts both a rational and irrational standpoint. He makes sure that when he is adopting the rational standpoint he is more passionate and more vigorous in his arguments than when he is adopting the irrational standpoint. This method which Burns (1980) has called externalisation of voices, can also be conducted by the client using a tape recorder.

Other emotive techniques that the client can employ himself involve an additional behavioural element. Thus, for example, the client can undertake various SHAME-ATTACKING EXERCISES for which RET is famous. The purpose of shame-attacking exercises is for the client to gain practice of

doing something which he would ordinarily experience as 'shameful'. In doing so he provides
himself with an opportunity to accept himself for
the 'shameful' act. Shame-attacking exercises also
provide information concerning other people's
reactions to the client's 'shameful' behaviour and
thus provide the client with information which may
correct any inaccurate inferences that the client
may have made. Shame-attacking exercises have
traditionally involved such tasks as standing in a
lift facing other passengers, taking a banana for a
walk and selling yesterday's newspapers. The
therapist had better make sure before the client
initiates such a technique that the client will not
get himself into trouble at work or with the police
and that the planned procedure will not
unnecessarily alarm or inconvenience other people
in his environment.

A similar, but perhaps less dramatic,
technique is the RISK-TAKING EXERCISE. Here clients
are encouraged to take risks that they might
ordinarily avoid. The client is prepared in advance
by the therapist who helps him identify and correct
self-defeating beliefs before he initiates such
risk-taking exercises. Examples of risk-taking
exercises are: returning slightly damaged goods or
asking a waiter to provide a new set of clean
cutlery. Risk-taking exercises, in general,
involve the client disputing beliefs concerning
dire need for approval. Another newly developed
emotive tecnique is the 'STEP OUT OF CHARACTER'
exercise. The client is asked to identify ways of
behaving or relating that he would ideally like to
adopt but which involves a step out of character for
him. Again the client is prepared cognitively
before he embarks on such an exercise.

These three exercises often involve the client
confronting his discomfort anxiety which involves
such irrational evaluations as 'I have to be
comfortable in doing something and I can't stand
being uncomfortable'. Since these exercises
involve the client in confronting his discomfort
anxiety, they can additionally be viewed as
exercises in raising a client's level of frustration
tolerance.

2.2.2.3 Behavioural methods. There are some
proponents of RET who claim that one of the best
ways a client can change his beliefs is by
behaviourally contradicting them. However, when
the client initiates acting in a new way or confronting a situation that he has previously avoided,

he is also practicing in-vivo cognitive disputing
since he is encouraged to enter the situation while
rehearsing rational self-statements. Since the
purpose of such behavioural techniques is to effect
cognitive changes, rational-emotive therapists
prefer to suggest to clients that they confront
situations that they wish to avoid, such as their
own anxiety or rejection, as well as suggesting that
they expose themselves to situations that they would
like, for example, acceptance. Thus common
behavioural homework exercises that clients often
initiate are ones that expose themselves to
potential rejection, a situation which will provide
them with a golden opportunity for showing
themselves (1) that they can stand rejection,
(2) that such rejection does not mean that they are
less of a person, and (3) that rejection is not an
'awful' experience. Needless to say the therapist
had better prepare the client for this somewhat
unorthodox type of homework assignment. In other
words, the therapist needs to clarify the rationale
behind such an assignment. Such behavioural
techniques are either designed to help clients raise
their level of frustration tolerance or to help them
to dispute ego-anxiety ideas. Behavioural
techniques that the client can initiate to raise
their level of frurstration tolerance include IN-
VIVO DESENSITIZATION whereby the client actually
goes out and confronts situations that he would
ordinarily avoid such as elevators, subway trains,
asking a woman to dance, etc. When employed as a
technique to raise clients level of frustration
tolerance, in-vivo desensitization is used in its
'flooding' rather than a gradual form. However,
quite often clients simply refuse to directly and
implosively confront such feared situations and
prefer a more gradual desensitization approach.
While the rational-emotive therapist regards the
flooding paradigm as more 'elegant' (i.e. promoting
greater attitude change), she had better now allow
her own preferences to disregard the clients' own
desires. In other words she would do well not to
threaten the therapeutic alliance.

Grieger and Boyd (1980) have written about a
group of techniques which they call 'STAY IN THERE'
activities. These techniques are designed to help a
client put up with chronic rather than acute
discomfort, and as such, these activities are liable
to be better accepted and completed by clients.
Clients can also initiate ANTI-PROCRASTINATION
EXERCISES which are designed to help the client

start a task earlier rather than later, thus behaviourally disputing dire needs for comfort.

To encourage clients who wish to initiate such behavioural techniques but are doubtful as to whether they are able to go through with it, the rational-emotive therapist can employ REWARDS AND PENALTIES. For example, if a client says that he wishes to do an anti-procrastination exercise but doubts whether he will in practice, the therapist might help him to identify some everyday rewarding experience which he is wiling to forego until he completes the exercise. Furthermore, the therapist helps the client to identify a particularly unpleasant task that the client would do his utmost to avoid and gains the client's agreement to do that unpleasant task if he has not completed the anti-procrastination exercise by an appointed time. The client may fail to do the anti-procrastination exercise and refuse to initiate the reward-penalty technique. However, in cases such as these the therapist need do no more than to remind the client of his responsibility for that choice and can help the client tolerate better the consequences of that choice.

Rational-emotive therapists indeed draw upon many techniques that behaviour therapists employ although their objectives may be different than the latter group. Thus, for example, the rational-emotive therapist might employ STIMULUS CONTROL with a client who finds it difficult to control eating behaviour. The therapist might suggest to the client that he initiate eating only in certain rooms and at certain times. The purpose here is to change the client's cognitions from 'I cannot control my eating' to 'I can control my eating'. When employing behavioural techniques, clients had better understand that the more frequently they initiate such techniques the faster they are likely to improve and as such the rate of their improvement is in their control.

3. ASSESSMENT OF PROGRESS

It is a good idea for therapists to continually monitor client's progress and have clients monitor their own progress throughout the course of therapy. This may involve the therapist and client keeping joint records of the client's achievements in therapy. This can be done with reference to the client's problem list which should be updated throughout therapy. In addition, the therapist may set aside particular sessions to review the client's therapeutic progress and if necessary re-negotiate new goals and/or set a date for termination. Thus, for example, I set aside every tenth session in my work with clients as a review session and at that sesson the client and I formally share our experiences concerning our work together. The client had better understand tht the overall goal of any therapy, but in RET in particular, is the acquisition of a sense of competence and a set of skills that he can use in the future if any similar or new problems should emerge rather than the eradication of emotional problems.

Some therapists, as clients improve, suggest that they meet less frequently, whereas other therapists prefer to meet regularly for a period of time and then set a termination date. I suggest that the therapist and client negotiate the approach which suits the client's own individual require-ments, rather than have the therapist impose a fixed and unchangeable policy. No matter what method of working towards termination is employed, it is wise for the therapist to schedule, if possible, a number of follow-up meetings where the client can meet with the therapist to review on-going progress after the termination of formal therapy sessions. At these sessions issues such as relapse can be addressed. Indeed, it may be wise prior to formal termination, for the therapist and client to spend a couple of sessions discussing the issue of relapse so that the client is prepared for such an evantuality, is not discouraged by its occurrence, and knows what to do in the face of its occurrance.

CONCLUSION

The purpose of this paper has been to show that for RET to be effective both therapist and client need to discharge their responsibilities. RET is a non-mystical therapy where therapists openly talk about techniques, their rationale and purpose. It is the therapist's responsibility to form an effective working alliance with the client, to present the structure of the therapy in such a way that the client can understand and agree with the major tasks of each participant. Furthermore the therapist's responsibiity is to employ as many techniques as is deemed appropriate to help the client to achieve his goals. However, no matter how competent a rational-emotive therapist may be, she can only help the client to achieve his goals if the client also understands and is prepared to meet his responsibilities. These responsibilities lie mainly in the area of putting into practice the insights that he has gained from therapy sessions and to develop the outlook that ongoing improvement requires ongoing work to consolidate change. When both parties are willing and able to discharge their responsibilities, it is my hypothesis tht rational-emotive therapy is truly effective!

NOTES

1. Through this chapter the therapist is referred to as 'she' and the client as 'he'.
2. Nathan Leopold along with Richard Loeb committed the 'crime of the century' in the 1920s by kidnapping and killing a young boy. Years later, Leopold was pardoned as a changed person, became a social worker, married and spent much of the rest of his life doing good work (Wessler and Wessler, 1980, p. 126).

PART TWO: INNOVATIONS

Chapter Three

RATIONAL-EMOTIVE THERAPY AND COGNITIVE THERAPY: A
CRITICAL COMPARISON

_____

A   critical   comparison   is   made   between
rational-emotive   therapy   and   cognitive   therapy.
The two approaches are compared as to their development,   their   theoretical   and   philosophical   underpinnings and their practical components.   It is
argued   that while rational-emotive therapy through
the writings of Albert Ellis has a more thoroughly
developed   philosophical   framework,   cognitive
therapy's strengths based on Aaron Beck's work, lie
in   the   explicit   practical   guidelines   that
therapists are offered.   There are signs that both
approaches   are   having   mutual   impact   and   closer
collaboration   is   recommended   between   rational-
emotive and cognitive therapists to enhance this
recent development.

_____

In   endeavouring to make a critical comparison
between   two approaches to psychotherapy, a writer
must make clear at the outset to which sources of
data he is referring in his comparative analysis.
In   comparing   rational-emotive   therapy   with   cognitive therapy I have utilised: (1) the writings of
both Aaron Beck and Albert Ellis, (2) other statements by Beck and Ellis which have not appeared in
publication form, (3) the views of experienced and
highly trained rational-emotive therapists and cognitive therapists, and (4) my own views concerning
the differences and similarities between rational-
emotive therapy and cognitive therapy based on my
experiences of being trained at both the Institute
for Rational-Emotive Therapy in New York and the
Center for Cognitive Therapy in Philadelphia.   My
aim in this comparative review is to consider both

approaches' (a) developmental history, (b) theoretical and philosophical underpinnings, and
(c) practical components.

At the outset it is important to note that
Ellis (1979f, 1980a) states that there are two forms
of RET: general RET which he claims is synonymous
with cognitive-behaviour therapy (Ellis, 1980a),
and specialised RET which he claims differs from CBT
in several important aspects[1]. I shall endeavour to
make clear at various junctures to which form of RET
I am referring in this paper.

1. <u>DEVELOPMENT</u>

Both rational-emotive therapy and cognitive
therapy were developed as a result of their
founders' dissatisfaction with psychoanalytic
theory and practice. However, while Ellis has
developed RET mainly outside the formal academic
arena, Beck has remained firmly within it. This
factor may partially account for the different
emphases apparent in the work of Beck and Ellis.
Ellis used to be in private practice and is now
Executive Director of two non-profit making
institutes. The Institute for Rational-Emotive
Therapy has a clinic where lengthy diagnostic interviews are not carried out. Over the years, Ellis
and his colleagues have seen patients representing
the broad spectrum of emotional disorders. RET,
then, has developed without Ellis and his colleagues
focusing on any one specific emotional disorder for
special and intensive empirical study and without
them carrying out rigorously designed outcome
studies. Beck and his colleagues, on the other
hand, have spent much of their time and attention
studying the psychological processes of the
depressive disorders and have carried out
rigorously designed outcome studies on the cognitive therapy of depression. Beck and his team are
now adopting a similar approach to the study of
anxiety disorders. In their clinic lengthy
diagnostic interviews are carried out.

These differences I think are reflected in the
different emphases found in Beck's and Ellis'
writings. Ellis has written extensively on a wide
variety of psychotherapeutic issues and the whole
spectrum of the emotional disorders. He has
recently written widely on the philosophical and
theoretical underpinnings of RET (e.g. Ellis, 1976,
1978, 1979a), has steadily over the years published
books and articles on the <u>general</u> strategy and

specific techniques used in RET (e.g. Ellis, 1958, 1962, 1968, 1971, 1975, 1979e) but somewhat surprisingly has not written much on the practice of RET over the course of treatment. He has recently published a treatment manual, twenty-three years after the inception of RET (Ellis and Abrahms, 1978).

In contrast, Beck's writings lack the breadth and variety of Ellis', but reflect the in-depth study replete with his own group's experimental work which is lacking in the work of Ellis (e.g. Beck, 1963, 1964, 1967, 1973; Beck et al., 1979). Beck (1976) has written a more general text on the emotional disorders but on closer inspection focuses mainly on the depressive and anxiety disorders. In this publication anger is covered only briefly while shame and guilt are not given coverage. Beck has not written extensively on the philosophical underpinnings of cognitive therapy but unlike Ellis has written on the practice of cognitive therapy over the course of treatment and has published three treatment manuals where therapeutic style, strategy and technique are specifically described.

Any comparison between rational-emotive therapy and cognitive therapy had better be placed in a historical context which illustrates the different interests and emphases in the work of the founding fathers. These differences do in my opinion account for some of the differences in the current status of the two approaches.

2.   THEORETICAL AND PHILOSOPHICAL UNDERPINNINGS

2.1   Images of the Person and the Acquisition of Emotional Disturbance

All approaches to psychotherapy are based on either explicit or implicit images of human beings. Such images do have a direct influence on the practice of therapy although such a relationship is of course confounded by other variables. Ellis (1976, 1978, 1979a) has spelled out in detail the image of the person which underlies his practice of specialised RET. In contrast, Beck does not address himself to this issue in his writings, preferring to focus on the theoretical and experimental factors associated with depression and anxiety.

Ellis (e.g. 1976, 1978) has consistently emphasised the biological basis of irrationality which he claims underlies most emotional disturbance. Indeed he writes:

"RET-oriented personality theory hypothesises that probably 80 per cent of the variance of human behaviour rests on biological bases and about 20 per cent on environmental training" (Ellis, 1978, p. 304).

It is difficult to determine to what extent this view is shared by rational-emotive therapists and to what extent adhering to this viewpoint influences therapeutic practice[2].

Beck's (1967, 1976) earlier work appeared to emphasise important early learning experiences in the development of cognitive schemas which leave a person vulnerable to emotional disorders. However in his more recent work, more emphasis is given to the influence of premorbid personality (Beck, 1983) and biological factors (Beck, 1982) in the development of emotional disorders.

Both Ellis and Beck have made similar statements concerning the acquisition of emotional disturbance. Ellis (1978, 1979a) considers there to be a multiplicity of origins of personality and presumably of emotional disturbance. In the same vein, Beck (in press) argues that it is counterproductive to speak of the cause of the affective disorders. He argues that there are a host of possible predisposing and precipitating factors in the development of depression. While making similar statements concerning the acquisition of emotional disturbance, it is clear that Beck and Ellis differ in their views concerning the ultimate determinants of emotional disturbance with Ellis stressing biological factors and Beck stressing significant learning experiences albeit against the background of a specific biological disposition (Herman, 1981, personal communication). Such differences show up in how Beck and Ellis talk about the development of emotional disturbance. While Beck talks and writes in terms of human beings learning dysfunctional underlying assumptions, Ellis talks in terms of human beings teaching themselves irrational beliefs (and being biologically prone to do so). A common Ellis message to his patients is:

"It's got zero to do with your mother and father, you taught yourself that nonsense".

While this phrase is an overexaggeration due to the point which Ellis wishes to make, it does capture his distaste for theories which make significant learning experiences primary in explaining the development of emotional disturbance.

While Ellis stresses humans' biological tendency towards irrationality, he however has an optimistic view of human potential for change.

"People . . . have an unusual capacity to change their cognitive and behavioral processes so that they can (a) choose to react differently from the way they usually do, (b) refuse to upset themselves about almost anything that may occur, and (c) train themselves so that they can semi-automatically remain minimally disturbed for the rest of their lives" (Ellis, 1979d, p. 2).

Thus, as we shall see, if human beings apply themselves they can achieve considerable results. While Beck, a priori, must have faith in the ability of humans to overcome their emotional problems, he has not written about this potential for change. However, it is difficult for me to imagine him writing in the same vein as Ellis. While Beck's view on this issue seems to me to be a traditional one i.e. human beings can achieve a fair measure of emotional health, while overcoming significant barriers, Ellis' view is less traditional, i.e. human beings can achieve a considerable measure of emotional health while overcoming gigantic barriers.

2.2 The Nature of Emotional Disturbance

Both Beck and Ellis have acquired their reputations for giving cognitive factors primacy in accounting for emotional disturbance and both stress that cognitions, feelings and behaviours inter-relate. In addition, both point to underlying cognitive structures as being at the root of emotional disturbance. However, they do not agree as to the nature of these underlying cognitive structures. For Ellis the root of emotional disturbance is a set of "musturbatory ideologies" towards self, others and life conditions in general (Ellis, 1977a). Such ideologies take the form of evaluations (as opposed to inferences) (Wessler and Wessler, 1980; Wessler, 1982b) and are absolutistic and grandiose in nature. Ellis calls these structures ideologies because he wishes to stress their philosophical nature. Such ideologies, claims Ellis, are responsible for the inferential cognitive distortions that Beck et al. (1979) so carefully document although this claim has yet to be studied. Beck (Beck et al., 1979; Kovacs and Beck, 1978) agrees that maladaptive underlying cognitive structures are responsible for patients' cognitive distortions about one's self, experiences and future, but does not agree with Ellis that these underlying assumptions or cognitive schema are invariably "musturbatory" and evaluative in nature. Beck (1976) does say that these assumptions tend to be absolute in nature as well as being characterized by such distortions as exaggeration and overgeneralization. Beck (1976, pp. 255-256) gives nine examples of underlying assumptions that pre-dispose people to depression. While seven of these assumptions are evaluative in nature, two are infer-ential statements about reality (i.e. 'If somebody disagrees with me, it means he doesn't like me' and 'If I don't take advantage of every opportunity to advance myself, I will regret it later'). This list is also quoted in Beck et al. (1979) and Coleman and Beck (1981) so it is possible to argue that this is still Beck's viewpoint. Thus we see that whereas rational-emotive therapists tend to clearly dis-tinguish between inferential (or what Ellis calls observations) and evaluative processes (Wessler and Wessler, 1980; Wessler, 1982b), cognitive therapists do not make such a clear distinction.

Ellis' viewpoint on emotional disturbance is centred around two basic themes. These I call "Ego Disturbance" and "Discomfort Disturbance". Emotional disturbance is due to human beings' failure to acknowledge or accept their human fallibility and their failure to adopt a tolerant attitude towards discomfort. Thus, Ellis tends to view disturbance in terms of two fundamental processes. Although Beck and other cognitive therapists (Beck et al., 1979; Burns, 1980) outline a number of faulty information processing styles or cognitive distortions which are reflected in under-lying assumptions, they tend to emphasize the idiosyncratic nature of these assumptions and do not specify such distinct fundamental processes. Thus while rational-emotive therapists tend to think in terms of finite clusters of irrational beliefs, cognitive therapists tend to think in terms of an infinite number of underlying assumptions (Herman, 1981, personal communication)[3].

Another difference between rational-emotive therapy and cognitive therapy which is derived from the writings of Beck and Ellis and my observations is that Ellis clearly distinguishes between what he calls appropriate and inappropriate emotions and cognitive therapists in general do not. For example, Ellis (1977d) in reviewing Beck's (1976) 'Cognitive Therapy and the Emotional Disorders' notes that Beck uses 'sadness' "as a term for all kinds of states ranging from mild regret to severe self-damning" (p. 295)[4,5]. Ellis' clear distinction between appropriate and inappropriate feelings stems from his clear distinction between 'healthy' rational beliefs and 'unhealthy' irrational beliefs. While no comparatively simple criteria have been described in the cognitive therapy literature for distinguishing between dys-functional and functional underlying assumptions, Young, a cognitive therapist, (1982, personal com-munication) does (as we shall see) employ criteria for distinguishing between functional and dys-functional thoughts, feelings and behaviours.

Ellis in his writings (e.g. Ellis, 1979a; Ellis and Abrahms, 1978) emphasizes that humans often disturb themselves about their disturbance and this is a significant feature of both his theory and his practice. While cognitive therapists acknowledge the prevalence of this process in anxiety disorders (i.e. anxiety about anxiety) the corresponding process in depression (i.e. depression about depression) is not prominently featured.

Beck and cognitive therapists, on the other hand, highlight inferential cognitive distortions prominently in their ideas about disturbance and as targets for change in their practical inter-ventions. For example, in depression, negative predictions about the future are regarded as a primary factor in depression and highly influential in the production of suicidal ideations. Ellis does acknowledge the influence of such distortions but these do not occupy a central role in his theorizing and practice.

2.3 Perpetuation of Emotional Disturbance

Beck et al. (1979) argue that depressed persons perpetuate their pain-inducing and self-defeating attitudes despite objective evidence of positive features in their lives. They argue that humans utilise cognitive schemata and faulty information-processing styles to edit out various potentially disconfirming experiences and distort such ex-periences to fit in with the activated cognitive schema. As a result alternatives are not explored and new behaviours not attempted. Thus, the person is likely to have familiar experiences which further perpetuate his disturbance (Herman, 1981, personal communication). While Ellis would not disagree with this view, his arguments concerning the perpetuation of emotional disturbance highlight the view that "most people have a natural tendency to resist basic personality change" (Ellis, 1979b, p. 51). He and Wessler (1978) argue that low frustration tolerance (LFT) is at the root of such perpetuation. We have already seen that cognitive therapists do not highlight this process in their writings. Ellis argues that most human beings have a natural affinity for comfort and thus opt for the relative comfort of short-term, self-defeating goals and in so doing miss out on the potential change-producing but uncomfortable experiences which striving for their long-term self-enhancing goals would afford.

2.4   The Nature of Emotional Health and Goals of Therapy

Ellis's image of the emotionally healthy individual is firmly rooted in a 'clinical-humanistic-atheistic' philosophy (Ellis, 1980b). His position is that if human beings are to experience emotional health they had better identify their self-enhancing life goals and work consistently toward them. Furthermore he specifies the sub-goals that will enable humans to be successful in their primary goal. These are (1) self-interest, (2) social interest, (3) self-direction, (4) tolerance, (5) flexibility, (6) acceptance of uncertainty, (7) commitment, (8) scientific thinking, (9) self-acceptance, (10) risk-taking and (11) non-utopianism (Ellis, 1979b, pp. 55-57). Ellis considers that the goals of specialised rational-emotive therapy had better be directed to help patients achieve these eleven sub-goals, and thus help them achieve what he calls a "profound philosophic change", while recognizing that in a large number of cases the therapist will have to settle for more conservative goals as in general RET. Furthermore, Ellis states that a major goal of RET is to help patients use what he calls "the scientific method" in the future to test out hypotheses about self, others and the world.

Beck has not addressed himself in detail to describing the characteristics of emotionally healthy individuals. He does say, however, that cognitive therapy techniques are designed to help people "identify, reality test and correct mal-adaptive distorted conceptualizations and the dys-functional beliefs (schemas) underlying those cog-nitions" (Beck et al., 1979, p.4). Emotionally healthy individuals are presumably, then, viewed as highly adept at such skills. From this, the goal of cognitive therapy can be seen as helping patients acquire and develop such skills - which is, in my opinion, more ambitious than Beck's subsequent statement: "the goal of cognitive therapy is to relieve emotional distress and the other symptoms of depression" (Beck et al., 1979, p.35).

It is doubtful that cognitive therapists generally adhere to a well-organised common philosophical position and consequently do not specify an equivalent list of subgoals. It is doubtful that they would have such aspirations. Indeed as Young (1982, personal communication) says, cognitive therapists place much more emphasis on modifying expectations than changing philosophies. At times cognitive therapists share Ellis' views on self-acceptance i.e. that a person had better accept himself not rate himself, but as Ellis has pointed out, they do not consistently take this position (Ellis, 1977d). However, implicit in their writings is the high regard given to the value of (a) realistic thinking and (b) functionality of thoughts, behaviours and emotions which may prove to be the cornerstones of any future theorizing concerning the philosophical underpinnings of cognitive therapy. Young (1982, personal communication) adopts two major criteria in helping patients determine the functionality of their thoughts, feelings and behaviours: (1) is it causing the patient unwanted symptoms? and (2) is it hurting others unnecessarily? The overlap between this concept of functionality and Ellis' concept of rationality which he defines as that which aids and abets one's long-term goals of survival and happiness is apparent.

2.5 Views on Change Processes

Both Beck and Ellis agree that for thorough-going cognitive change, repeated rethinking and responding to dysfunctional cognitions is necessary. However, while Ellis argues that therapists had better help patients do this forcefully and energetically, Beck does not address himself directly to the issue of force in any of his writings. By implication, however, force is not advocated within the therapeutic style of collaborative empiricism which as we shall see is one of the hallmarks of cognitive therapy. Burns (1980), a cognitive therapist, however, does describe and uses freely a technique which he calls 'externalization of voices'[6] which does require patients to respond to their own dysfunctional cognitions in an energetic manner.

While both Beck and Ellis stress the importance of behaviour change in effecting cognitive change,

48

Beck and other cognitive therapists have traditionally advocated helping patients to try out new behaviours in a graded fashion being careful not to expose them to undue discomfort. Cognitive change is deemed to occur when the patient processes and integrates the outcome of these behavioural assignments which are likely to be designed to test out his hypotheses. Ellis is likely to favour behavioural assignments which repeatedly expose patients "at a jump" to uncomfortable and feared situations arguing that for patients who will do it, these experiences bring about the greatest amount of cognitive change and help patients raise their level of frustration tolerance. Since, as we shall see, cognitive therapists value highly the stance of 'collaborative empiricism', they are likely to negotiate behavioural assignments which the patient feels he is able to handle. These are unlikely to be too demanding. It is my experience that a number of rational-emotive therapists adopt this approach rather than that of Ellis.

However, Beck, in very recent writings on shame, advocates that the person needs to have "shameful" experiences in order to begin to see that such experiences are tolerable. Furthermore in a recent statement, Beck (1982, personal communication) has said that while graded task assignments are recommended for use with depressed patients, exposure assignments are more effective with anxious patients. (Thus there seems to be a rapproachement in viewpoints on this issue).

3.   PRACTICAL ISSUES

    3.1 Therapeutic Style
    A variety of RET therapists have made the point that it is not necessary to adopt Ellis' forceful style with most patients in order to practice effective RET (Walen et al., 1980; Wessler and Wessler, 1980) and Ellis himself does acknowledge that RET can be practiced in many different styles, including one normally associated with client-centred therapists. However, Ellis (1979c) does consider that the preferred therapeutic style of rational-emotive therapists is one that emphasises both active-directiveness and therapeutic forcefulness. One main reason why Ellis advocates forcefulness as a preferred therapeutic style is due to his belief that there is a strong biological basis to human irrationality that had better be forcefully combatted. In contrast, while Beck

stresses that in the short-term treatment of depressed patients, active-directiveness is a preferred style, collaboration, rather than confrontation, is to be regarded as one of the most important hallmarks of cognitive therapy. Indeed as Young and Beck (1982) say, "cognitive therapy . . . consists of a particular therapeutic <u>style</u>, as well as a set of techniques". This therapeutic style is called '<u>collaborative empiricism</u>'. The stance of collaborative empiricism is one in which the therapist ensures that he explains to the patient the rationale for everything that he does. Patient and therapist set an agenda at every session. The therapist helps the patient identify and question maladaptive cognitions through guided discovery. He frequently pauses and asks for feedback from patients to determine the impact of his therapeutic interventions, and basically clues patients into whatever is happening in the therapeutic endeavour. This style has influenced the practice of some rational-emotive therapists (e.g. Wessler and Wessler, 1980). Whenever I have heard Ellis' therapy sessions, while he does endeavour to develop a collaborative relationship with his clients, he does not by this definition adhere to the stance of collaborative empiricism. Ellis (1981, personal communication) has said that with patients who are relatively undisturbed and non-defensive, it is possible to take such a stance in RET, but he would like to know exactly how Beck and his colleagues deal with what he calls "difficult customers", namely the resistant, disturbed and defensive clients, which he says constitute the bulk of his clinical case-load. He hypothesises that adopting the collaborative empirical stance with such patients would have less effect than adopting a forceful stance. Young (1982, personal communication) however, has said that with patients who are particularly rigid in their thinking a confrontative style can be employed in cognitive therapy when collaborative empiricism has been exhausted. Such a confrontative style is used, however, as a last resort.

3.2 <u>Therapeutic strategy</u>

Rational-emotive therapists and cognitive therapists differ in the speed with which therapists and patients move towards the identification and modification of underlying maladaptive assumptions. In cognitive therapy the initial task of the therapist in dealing with a patient's cognitions is to help him identify and correct his automatic thoughts. These thoughts are ones which the patient can identify first and constitute the tip of the cognitive iceberg. This is repeated until tentative hypotheses can be developed concerning both secondary and primary assumptions which underlie these automatic thoughts. These hypotheses are either confirmed or rejected as the result of the collection of more data. Such an approach is lengthy and is usually reserved for the middle to later stages of therapy. This entire procedure is based on the principle of <u>induction</u> since the cognitive therapist does not claim to know at the outset the nature of the patient's cognitions which is centrally related to his emotional disturbance. He thus chips away from the outer layer of the automatic thoughts to the inner core of the basic assumption. On the other hand, Ellis claims that he can quickly discern the patient's cognitions which are centrally related to his problem: namely the absolutistic evaluations which are either couched in the form of a 'must' or in the form of a grossly exaggerated negative conclusion. Thus, it can be seen that Ellis is operating according to the principle of <u>deduction</u>. Ellis tends to refer to the patient's automatic thoughts (as defined by Beck) only briefly and as a means to identify these irrational beliefs. Thus, while Ellis is likely to go straight for the patient's evaluative thinking and then deal with any remaining inferential distortions after doing so, Beck and cognitive therapists in general are more likely to deal with inferential cognitive distortions initially and only later, if at all, deal with the patient's evaluative thinking. I say "if at all" because, as we have seen, patients' primary underlying assumptions do not in cognitive therapy necessarily take the form of evaluations. I would hypothesise that this difference is a distinguishing feature between rational-emotive therapists and cognitive therapists in general.

While I have outlined differences between rational-emotive therapists' and cognitive therapists' typical strategic approaches, it is worth noting that rational-emotive therapists claim more leeway in deviating from the typical. In response to Beck et al.'s criticism of rational-emotive therapists that they often do not establish a solid data base against which the patient's conclusions can be tested, Ellis says that:

". . . although RET therapists are not required to do this as you seem to do it, they can easily choose to do so. In many instances I would proceed almost exactly as your therapists did in the dialogue given in this section of the manual; in other instances, I might possibly proceed to discussing the patient's worth or her catastrophising - and in the course of doing so derive the 'solid data base' information. In a few other cases, I might help her to fully accept herself or to stop catastrophising without the data base information brought out in your instance - but with various other kinds of information brought out. RET does <u>not</u> have one special way of questioning and disputing".

(Ellis quoted in Beck et al., 1979, p. 154). However, it is my view that in specialised RET, therapists would more likely proceed straight to patients' evaluative beliefs while in general RET, they could and often do proceed as cognitive therapists would. One of the major reasons why cognitive therapists do not deviate from a standardized sequence of treatment procedures is that their outcome studies require standardized treatment. However, both rational-emotive and cognitive therapists need to be more mindful of the question: "Is an early focus on inferential or evaluative cognitions likely to be more effective with this particular client?"

3.3 Therapeutic Techniques

There are a number of differences between rational-emotive therapists and cognitive therapists in their use of techniques. While Ellis claims that virtually every behavioural and cognitive technique that has ever been invented is used in general RET and thus presumably all the techniques that cognitive therapists have devised would fall under the rubric of general RET, I shall confine my statements to a comparison between specialised RET and cognitive therapy.

While both rational-emotive therapists and cognitive therapists make use of inductive questioning or the 'socratic dialogue' method, I have observed that cognitive therapists are likely to persist longer with this method than rational-emotive therapists. Rational-emotive therapists do tend to use explanations more frequently than do cognitive therapists and faced with patients who do not seem to benefit from the 'socratic dialogue' are likely to dispense with this method sooner than cognitive therapists.

Rational-Emotive Therapy and Cognitive Therapy

Both rational-emotive therapists and cognitive therapists are well-known for asking their patients to look for evidence for their irrational evaluations and faulty inferences respectively. However, and this is a feature of Ellis' practice in particular, rational-emotive therapists are likely to ask for evidence of statements where no corroborating evidence is likely to exist. Thus, when a rational-emotive therapist asks a patient: "Where is the evidence that you <u>must</u> succeed?", he knows a priori that there is in <del>all</del> probability no evidence that could corroborate such a statement. There are no behavioural experiments, for example, that a patient and therapist could construct, the results of which could in fact corroborate such a statement. Thus, rational-emotive therapists quite often ask patients for evidence concerning their irrational evaluations – matters which more appropriately belong to the realm of ideology[7]. These are questions which a patient can in fact answer while sitting in the therapist's armchair using reason alone. Ellis (1982, personal communication) has said that one main reason why he asks patients for evidence supporting their irrational beliefs is because patients often regard such beliefs as facts. On the other hand, cognitive therapists are more likely to ask patients for evidence concerning their inferences (hypotheses) where data can be gathered from the outside world to corroborate or falsify the hypotheses.

Thus, if a patient predicts that he will be laughed at when he walks into a room full of people, the cognitive therapist and patient can construct an experiment to test the validity of such a hypothesis. Cognitive therapists are not noted for asking patients for evidence concerning matters belonging to the realm of ideology. They prefer to limit their discussion of such matters to questioning patients concerning the functionality of adhering to such beliefs. Taking this example further, when a rational-emotive therapist asks the patient: "Where is the evidence that it would be terrible if you are laughed at?", he knows there is in all probability only one answer to this question. He can further show the patient in the session that there is in all probability only one answer. The patient can even acknowledge the 'correct' ideological position. However, paradoxically, the patient will probably only believe in the 'correct' ideological position if he practices adhering to the new position in the outside world.

In my observations of cognitive therapists, it seems to me that one of the most important technical procedures that they have in their armamentarium is the use of the Daily Record of Dysfunctional Thoughts (DRDT) form. This has been verified by Herman (1981, personal communication). By contrast, although there are a number of written homework forms that have been devised by rational-emotive therapists, these are neither employed consistently nor seen as a major therapeutic change agent. I believe this may be because rational-emotive therapists do not pay as much attention to the role of automatic thoughts in emotional disturbance as do cognitive therapists.

While both Beck and Ellis recommend the use of imagery techniques, Beck and other cognitive therapists employ a wider range of imagery methods than does Ellis who employs mainly rational-emotive imagery (Ellis and Abrahms, 1978) and sexual imagery in the treatment of sexual problems. However, other rational emotive therapists such as Wessler (Wessler and Wessler, 1980; Wessler, 1982a) are more similar to cognitive therapists in employing a wide variety of imagery procedures.

As we have seen, rational-emotive therapists and cognitive therapists are likely to favour different types of behavioural assignment. Cognitive therapists are more likely to employ behavioural assignments in the service of helping patients to test faulty inferences or hypotheses (for example, they can be used quite early on in the treatment of a severely withdrawn depressed patient who hypothesises that he could not read even a sentence of a book). Rational-emotive therapists, and Ellis in particular, are likely to employ behavioural assignments, primarily in the service of changing evaluations. As a result, such behavioural assignments often aim to recreate patients' worst fears so as to enable them to see that they can cope with the worst. As we have seen Ellis often advocates behavioural assignments based on the principle of flooding in order to help patients raise their level of frustration tolerance. He would criticise the use of graded behavioural assignments which are used in cognitive therapy particularly with depressed patients as often doing little to change a patient's philosophy of LFT. In fact he argues that such graded task assignments communicate the implicit message "Yes, you do need to go slowly, you cannot stand to expose yourself to more discomfort than this" (Ellis, 1983b).

Cognitive therapists would counter that to urge most patients (particularly those who are depressed) to full exposure would threaten the therapeutic alliance and be against the spirit of collaborative empiricism. However cognitive therapists and patients could very well negotiate flooding assignments if so desired within such collaborative guidelines. It is my impression, however, that they do not do so frequently although they aim to do this in their future work with anxious patients.

Since cognitive therapists adhere to the collaborative empiricism stance, this prohibits the use of certain techniques that rational-emotive therapists would employ. For example, paradoxical procedures are not advocated in cognitive therapy since the explanation of the rationale underlying a paradoxical procedure would in fact negate the impact of the procedure. Furthermore cognitive therapists are not encouraged to use the somewhat flamboyant and dramatic interventions rational-emotive therapists sometimes employ which, while possibly having a great amount of therapeutic impact for the patient, may backfire (Dryden, 1982b). In this regard rational-emotive therapists are greater risk-takers than cognitive therapists. In addition, rational-emotive therapists make more of a concerted effort to use humour in their interventions to help patients take life less seriously. As DiGiuseppe (1982, personal communication) has said, rational-emotive therapists are freer than cognitive therapists to use a wide range of educational and social psychological methods to help change maladaptive cognitions and beliefs.

Finally in the correction of maladaptive basic assumptions, cognitive therapists are likely to emphasize pragmatic arguments to help patients change the nature of these assumptions and are less likely than rational-emotive therapists to help patients see the philosophical errors inherent in their assumptions. Rational-emotive therapists use both pragmatic and philosophical arguments in helping patients to give up their irrational beliefs.

4. CONCLUSION

Rational-emotive therapy's strengths lie in the fact that it is based on a well developed and well articulated set of philosophical formulations provided primarily by Albert Ellis. Until very recently, rational-emotive therapists have not had recourse to a treatment manual and even now such guidelines as have been provided in these manuals (Ellis and Abrahms, 1978; Walen et al., 1980) lack the specificity of those provided for cognitive therapists (e.g. in Beck et al., 1979), especially over the whole course of therapy.

Cognitive therapy's strengths lie in the careful work that has gone into the development of clear and precise treatment manuals which can be used in outcome studies. It's weaknesses lie in the fact that such practical advances have far out-stripped the development of its philosophical underpinnings. This could be a focus for future work.

There are signs that rational-emotive therapists are being influenced by the activities of Beck and his colleagues and also vice versa. In my opinion, one of the strengths of cognitive therapy has been the careful attention that Beck and his colleagues have paid to maximising the use of valuable therapeutic time. Thus agenda setting, careful attention to the development and main-tenance of the collaborative working alliance are features which some rational-emotive supervisors are now encouraging their supervisees to employ (Walen et al., 1980; Wessler and Wessler, 1980). Conversely it is my hypothesis that as cognitive therapists adopt the same careful study of anxiety disorders as they have of depressive disorders, they will, and there is some evidence that this is already happening, learn the value of encouraging patients to take greater behavioural risks in over-coming one of the major bases of anxiety disorders, that is discomfort anxiety. Indeed I believe that cognitive therapists have a lot to learn from Albert Ellis about discomfort anxiety, and there are signs that they are beginning to do so. This process of mutual influence will continue given greater contact between rational-emotive therapists and cognitive therapists.

ACKNOWLEDGEMENTS

I am grateful to the following people with whom I discussed some of the issues which appear in this paper and/or who gave feedback on earlier drafts: Aaron T. Beck, Ray DiGiuseppe, Albert Ellis, Art Freeman, Ray Harrison, Ira Herman, George Lockwood, Sue Walen, Richard Wessler, Ruth Wessler, and Jeff Young. However, only the author is responsible for the paper's content.

NOTES

1. These ways are "Cognitively, it has a pro-
    nounced philosophic emphasis, includes a
    humanistic-existentialist outlook, strives for
    pervasive and long-standing rather than
    symptomatic change, tries to eliminate all
    self-ratings, stresses antimusturbatory rather
    than antiempirical disputing methods,
    recognizes the palliative aspects of cognitive
    distraction, discourages problem solving that
    is not accompanied by changes in clients' basic
    belief system, and emphasizes secondary as
    well as primary symptoms of emotional dis-
    turbance. Emotively it stresses the dis-
    crimination of appropriate from inappropriate
    emotions, emphasizes methods of working
    directly with and on emotions, encourages
    forceful emotive interventions, and uses rel-
    ationship procedues that heavily stress un-
    conditional rather than conditional positive
    regard. Behaviorally, it favors penalization
    as well as reinforcement, is partial to in vivo
    desensitization and flooding and makes sure
    that skill training is done within a
    philosophic framework of trying to help
    clients make basic changes in their irrational
    beliefs" (Ellis, 1980a).
2. Throughout this paper it should be noted that
    the extent to which rational-emotive
    therapists and cognitive therapists agree with
    the views expressed by Ellis and Beck
    respectively is not known. This remains a
    fruitful area for research.
3. Herman's view has recently been challenged by
    Freeman (1982, personal communication) who
    claims that cognitive therapists think in
    terms of finite clusters of underlying
    assumptions, while acknowledging their idio-
    syncratic nature.
4. Beck (1982, personal communication) says that
    Ellis has misinterpreted him on this point.
5. Burns (1980), however, does distinguish bet-
    ween sadness and depression.
6. Alternatively called the "point-counter point"
    technique (Young, 1982, personal com-
    munication).
7. Here it is again to be noted that Ellis (1977a)
    refers to such irrational evaluations as
    "ideologies".

Chapter Four

VIVID RET I: RATIONALE AND PROBLEM ASSESSMENT

The fundamental goal of rational-emotive
therapy is to enable clients to live effective lives
by helping them change their faulty inferences and
irrational evaluations about themselves, other
people and the world. While there are many ways of
achieving this goal, the purpose of chapters 4, 5
and 6 is to highlight the ways in which rational-
emotive therapists can make the therapeutic process
a more vivid experience for their clients so that
they may be stimulated to more effectively identify
and change their faulty inferences and irrational
evaluations. A number of rational-emotive and
cognitive therapists have already written on the use
of vivid methods in therapy (Arnkoff, 1981; Ellis,
1979e; Freeman, 1981; Knaus and Wessler, 1976;
Walen, DiGiuseppe and Wessler, 1980 and Wessler and
Wessler, 1980). However, a comprehensive account of
the uses, advantages and limitations of such methods
has yet to appear in the literature on rational-
emotive therapy. The aim of chapters 4, 5 and 6 is
to provide such an account. In this chapter,
attention will be given to the use of vivid methods
in problem assessment. Chapter 5 will focus on
vivid disputing methods, while Chapter 6 will
feature vivid ways in which clients may work through
their emotional and behavioural problems.

1. RATIONALE FOR VIVID METHODS IN RET

Rational-emotive therapists aim to help
clients achieve their goals through the systematic
application of cognitive, emotive and behavioural
methods. However, therapist and client rely heavily
on verbal dialogue in their in-session encounters.
The tone of such dialogue in rational-emotive
therapy sessions can be rich, stimulating and

arousing but is far too often dry and mundane (as supervisors of novice rational-emotive therapists will testify). While the role of emotional arousal in the facilitation of attitude change is complex (Hoehn-Saric, 1978), it is my contention that the majority of clients can be best helped to re-examine faulty inferences and irrational beliefs if we as therapists gain their full attention and make therapy a memorable experience for them. While there are no studies that are addressed to this point in the rational-emotive therapy literature, there is some suggestion from process and outcome studies carried out on client-centred therapy that vivid therapist interventions are associated with successful client outcome and with certain client in-therapy behaviours which have in turn been linked to positive outcome (Rice, 1965; Rice, 1973; Rice and Gaylin, 1973; Rice and Wagstaff, 1967; Wexler, 1975; and Wexler and Butler, 1976). At present we do not know whether any client in-therapy behaviours are associated with successful outcome in RET. Yet, it is possible to hypothesize that such client in-session behaviours as attending to and being fully involved in the therapeutic process and making links between in-session dialogue and out-of-session activities will be associated with therapeutic gain in RET.   If this proves correct then it is my further contention that vivid methods in RET may more effectively bring about such client behaviour.

Given the dearth of much-needed studies on these points, anecdotal evidence will have to suffice. The idea of 'Vivid RET' was prompted by feedback from my clients who frequently related incidents of (1) how my own vivid therapeutic inter-ventions helped them to re-examine a variety of their dysfunctional cognitions and of (2) how they, with my encouragement, improved by making the working through process a more stimulating ex-perience for themselves.

It should be stressed at the outset that while there is a place for vivid methods in RET, these are best introduced into therapy at appropriate times and within the context of a good therapeutic alliance between therapist and client.

2.   PROBLEM ASSESSMENT

Effective rational-emotive therapy depends initially on the therapist gaining a clear under-standing of (1) the client's problems in cognitive, emotional and behavioural terms and (2) the

59

contexts in which the client's problems occur. To a great extent, therapist are dependent on the client's verbal reports to help him gain such an understanding. It is in this area that many obstacles to progress may appear. Some clients have great difficulty identifying and/or accurately labelling their emotional experiences. Other clients are in touch with and able to report their emotions but find it hard to relate these to activating events (either external or internal). Yet a further group of clients are easily able to report problematic activating events and emotional experiences but have difficulty seeing how these may relate to mediating cognitions. Vivid methods can be used in a variety of ways to overcome such obstacles to a valid and reliable assessment of client problems.

2.1 Vividness in Portraying Activating Events. With some clients, traditional assessment procedures through verbal dialogue do not always yield the desired information. When this occurs, rational-emotive therapists often use imagery methods. They ask clients to conjure up evocative images of activating events. Such evocative imagery often stimulates the clients' memories concerning their emotional reactions or indeed in some instances leads to the re-experiencing of these reactions in the session. While focusing on such images, the client can also begin to gain access to cognitive processes below the level of awareness which cannot be easily reached through verbal dialogue.

One particularly effective use of imagery in the assessment of client problems is that of bringing future events into the present. This is illustrated by the following exchange between myself and a client who was terrified that her mother might die which led her to be extremely unassertive with the mother.

Therapist: So you feel you just can't speak up to her. Because if you did, what might happen?

Client: Well, she might have a fit . . .

Therapist: And what might happen if she did?

Client: She might have a heart attack and die.

Therapist: Well we know that she is a fit woman, but let's go along with your fear for the moment. OK?

Client: OK.

Therapist:	What if she did die?
Client:	I just can't think . . . I . . . I'm sorry.
Therapist:	That's OK. I know this is difficult but I really think it would be helpful if we could get to the bottom of things. OK? (Client nods). Look, Marjorie, I want you to imagine that your mother has just died this morning. Can you imagine that? (Client nods and begins to shake). What are you experiencing?
Client:	When you said my mother was dead I began to feel all alone . . . like there was no-one to care for me . . . no-one I could turn to.
Therapist:	And if there is no one who cares for you, no-one you can turn to.
Client:	Oh God! I know I couldn't cope on my own.

Instructing clients to vividly imagine something that has been warded off often leads to anxiety itself. It is important to process this anxiety as it is sometimes related to the client's central problem. Issues like fear of loss of control, phrenophobia and extreme discomfort anxiety are often revealed when this anxiety is fully assessed. However, some clients do find it difficult to spontaneously imagine events and require therapist assistance.

While imagery methods are now routinely used in RET and cognitive behaviour therapy (e.g. Lazarus, 1978), there has been little written on how therapists can stimulate clients' imagery processes. I have used a number of vivid methods to try and help clients utilize their potential for imagining events:

(a) Vivid, Connotative Therapist Language. One effective way of helping clients to use their imagery potential is for the therapist to use rich, colourful and evocative language while aiding clients to set the scene. Unless the therapist has gained prior diagnostic information, he is sometimes uncertain about which particular stimuli in the activating event are particularly related to the client's problem. Thus, it is best to give clients many alternatives. For example, with a socially anxious client I proceeded thus after attempting to get him to use his own potential for imagery without success.

Therapist: So at the moment we are unclear about what you are anxious about. What I'd like to suggest is that we use your imagination to help us. I will help you set the scene based on what we have already discussed. However, since we have yet to discover detailed factors some of the things I say might not be relevant. Will you bear with me and let me know when what I say touches a nerve in you?

Client: OK.

Therapist: Fine.   Just close your eyes and imagine you are about to walk into the dance. You walk in and some of the guys there glance at you. You can see the <u>smirks</u> on their <u>mock-ing</u> faces and one of them <u>blows</u> you a kiss . . . (Here I am testing out a hypothesis based on pre-viously gained information) . . . you start to <u>seethe</u> inside and . . .

Client: OK, when you said I was starting to seethe, that struck a chord. I thought I can't let them get away with that but if I let go I'll just go crazy. I started feeling anxious.

Therapist: And if you went crazy?

Client: I couldn't show my face in there again.

Therapist: What would happen then?

Client: I don't know. I . . . It's funny the way I see it I would never go out again.

Here I was using words like "smirks, mocking, blows and seethe" deliberately in my attempt to stimulate the client's imagination.   It is also important for the therapist to vary his tone so that this matches the language employed.

(b)   <u>Photographs</u>.   I have at times asked clients to bring to interviews photographs of significant others or significant places.   These are kept to hand, to be used at relevant moments in the assessment process.   I have found the use of photographs particularly helpful when the client is discussing an event in the past that is still bothering him.   Thus, for example, one client who spoke without feeling about being rejected by his

62

father who died seven years hence, broke down in tears when I asked him to look at a picture of him and his father standing apart from one another. Feelings of hurt and anger (with their associated cognitions) were expressed which enabled us to move to the disputing stage.

(c) <u>Other Momentoes</u>. In similar vein, I have sometimes asked clients to bring in momentoes. These may include pictures they have drawn, paintings that have meaning for them and poems either written by themselves or other people. The important point is that these momentoes are to be related to issues that the client is working on in therapy. A roadblock to assessment was successfully overcome with one client when I asked her to bring in a momento which reminded her of her mother. She brought in a bottle of perfume which her mother was accustomed to wearing. When I asked her to smell the perfume at a point in therapy when the assessment process through verbal dialogue was again breaking down, the client was helped to identify feelings of jealousy towards her mother which she experienced whenever her mother left her to go out socialising. Moreover, my client was ashamed of such feelings. This issue was centrally related to her presenting problem of depression.

Another of my clients was depressed about losing her boyfriend. I had great difficulty helping her to identify any related mediating cognitions through traditional assessment procedures. Several tentative guesses on my part also failed to pinpoint relevant cognitive processes. I then asked her to bring to our next session anything that reminded her of her ex-boyfriend. She brought in a record of a popular song that had become known as "our song". When I played the song to her at an appropriate point in the interview, my client began to sob and expressed feelings of abandonment, hurt and fear for the future. Again a vivid method had unearthed important assessment material where traditional methods had failed.

It should be noted from the above examples that quite often such dramatic methods lead to the expression of strong affective reactions in the session. This is often an important part of the process because such affective reactions are gate-ways to the identification of maladaptive cognitive processes which are difficult to identify through more traditional methods of assessment. In this respect Ellis (personal communication) notes that

Gendlin's (1978) focusing technique is often highly
effective in identifying clients' exact irrational
ideas by helping them to zero in on their feelings
and body sensations.

   (d)   The 'Interpersonal Nightmare Technique'.
Rational-emotive and cognitive therapists sometimes
employ methods originally derived from gestalt
therapy and psychodrama to assist them in the
assessment phase of therapy.   These have been
adequately described (Arnkoff, 1981; Nardi, 1979)
and will not be discussed here.   I would like to
describe a related technique which I have developed
(Dryden, 1980b) and which I call the 'Interpersonal
Nightmare Technique'.   This technique may be best
used with clients who are able to specify only
sketchily an anticipated 'dreaded' event involving
other people but are neither able to specify in any
detail the nature of the event nor how they would
react if the event were to occur.   First, the client
is given a homework assignment to imagine the
'dreaded' event.   He is told to write a brief
segment of a play about it, specifying the exact
words that the protagonists would use.   The client
is encouraged to give full vein to his imagination
while focusing on what he fears might happen.   An
example will suffice.   The following scenario was
developed by a 55 year-old woman with drink problems
who was terrified of making errors at the office
where she worked as a typist.
Scene:
Boss's office where he sits behind a very large
desk.   He has found out that one of the typists had
inadvertantly filed a letter wrongly, and sends for
her.   She comes in and is made to stand in front of
the Boss:

   Boss: Have you anything to say in this
                  matter?
   Typist(me):   Only that I apologise and will be
                  more careful in future.
   Boss: What do you mean by saying you will
                  be more careful in future; what
                  makes you think you have a future?
                  (At this point he starts banging
                  on the desk).   I have never yet met
                  anyone less competent or less
                  suited to the job than you are.
                  You mark my words, I will make life
                  so uncomfortable that you will
                  leave.   When I took over this job I
                  intended to have the people I
                  wanted working for me and you are

not on that list.   I have already
got rid of two typists and I shall
see that you are the third.   Now
get out of my office you stupid,
blundering fool and remember I
shall always be watching you and
you will never know when I shall be
behind you.
I then read over the scene with the client,
making enquiries concerning the tone in which she
thought her boss would make these statements and
asking her to identify which words the boss would
emphasize.   I then arranged for a local actor who
was the same age as the boss to realistically enact
the scene on cassette.   In the next session I
instructed my client to visualize the room in which
the encounter might take place.   She briefly
described the room paying particular attention to
where her boss would be sitting and where she would
be standing.   I then played her the cassette which
evoked strong feelings of fear of being physically
harmed and humiliated.   Again important data had
been collected which traditional assessment
procedures had failed to uncover.

The above examples have shown how rational-
emotive therapists can employ various visual,
olfactory, language and auditory methods to help
clients vividly imagine appropriate activating
events.   This in turn helps them more easily
identify maladaptive emotional experiences and
related cognitive processes which are not readily
identified through the verbal interchange of the
psychotherapeutic interview.   It is important to
note that the use of such methods is not being
advocated for their own sake.   They are employed
with specific purposes in mind.

2.2 Rational-Emotive Problem Solving.   Knaus
and Wessler (1976) have described a method which
they call rational-emotive problem solving (REPS).
This method involves the therapist creating
conditions in the therapy session which approximate
those that clients encounter in their everyday
situations and which give rise to emotional
problems.   Knaus and Wessler contend that this
method may be either used in a planned or impromptu
fashion and is particularly valuable when clients
experience difficulty in identifying emotional
experiences and related cognitive processes through
verbal dialogue with their therapists.   I employed
this method with a male client who reported
difficulty in acting assertively in his life and who

claimed not to be able to identify the emotions and thoughts which inhibited the expression of assertive responses. During our discussion I began to search around for my pouch of pipe tobacco. Finding it empty, I interrupted my client and asked him if he would drive to town, purchase my favourite tobacco, adding that if he hurried he could return for the last five minutes of our interview.   He immediately got up, took my money and walked out of my office towards his car.   I rushed after him, brought him back into my office and together we processed his reactions to this simulated experience!

It is clear that this technique must be used with therapeutic judgment and that its use may threaten or even destroy the therapeutic alliance between client and therapist.   However since rational-emotive therapists value risk-taking they are often prepared to take such risks when more traditional and less risky methods have failed to bring about therapeutic improvement. It is further important, as Beck et al. (1979) have stressed, for the therapist to ask clients for their honest reactions to this procedure, to ascertain whether it may have future therapeutic value for a particular client.   When a client indicates that he/she has found the rational-emotive problem solving method unhelpful, the therapist had better then explain his rationale for attempting such a procedure and disclose that he intended the client no harm but was attempting to be helpful. Normally clients respect such disclosures and in fact the therapist in doing so provides a useful model for the client: namely that it is possible to nondefensively acknowledge errors without damning oneself. However, with this method, it is apparent that therapists cannot realistically disclose the rationale in advance of initiating the method since this would detract from its potential therapeutic value.

2.3 Dreams.   Although Albert Ellis has recently written a regular column for "Penthouse" magazine, providing rational-emotive interpretations of readers' dreams, rational-emotive therapists are not generally noted for using dream material. However there is no good reason why dream material cannot be used in RET as long as (1) it does not predominate the therapeutic process and (2) the therapist has a definite purpose in mind in using it.

Freeman (1981) has outlined a number of further guidelines for the use of dreams for assessment purposes:
(1)   "The dream needs to be understood in thematic rather than symbolic terms . . .
(2)   The thematic content of the dream is idio-syncratic to the dreamer and must be viewed within the context of the dreamer's life . . .
(3)   The specific language and imagery are important to the meaning . . .
(4)   The affective responses to the dreams can be seen as similar to the dreamer's affective responses in waking situations . . .
(5)   The particular length of the dream is of lesser import than the content . . .
(6)   The dream is a product of and the res-ponsibility of the dreamer . . .
(7)   Dreams can be used when the patient appears stuck in therapy."
       (pp. 228-229).
I inadvertently stumbled on the usefulness of dream material for assessment purposes when working with a 28 year-old depressed student who would frequently reiterate: "I'm depressed and I don't know why".   I had virtually exhausted all the assessment methods I knew (including those des-cribed in this paper) to help her identify dep-ressogenic thoughts in situations when she experienced depression, but without success.   In a desperate last attempt, I asked her if she could remember any of her dreams, not expecting in the least that this line of enquiry would prove fruit-ful.   To my surprise she said yes, she did have a recurring dream.   In this dream she saw herself walking alone along a river bank and when she peered into the river, she saw a reflection of herself as a very old woman.   This image filled her with extreme sadness and depression.   On further discussion she said that she believed that this dream meant that she had no prospect of finding any happiness in her life, either in love relationships or in her career and that she was doomed to spend her years alone ending up as a sad, pathetic, old woman.   This account of the dream and subsequent discussion of its meaning enabled me to help her identify a number of inferential distortions and irrational beliefs which provided the focus for subsequent cognitive restructuring.
Daydreams may also provide important material for assessment purposes.   For some people, particular daydreams occur in response to and as

compensation for a negative activating event. Thus, one client reported having the daydream of establishing a multi-national corporation after failing to sell insurance to prospective customers. The use of such daydreams by clients may not necessarily be dysfunctional but may impede them (as in the above example) getting to the core of their problems. Often daydreams are an expression of our hopes and aspirations and I have found it valuable to not only ask clients about the content of such material but also what would stop them actualizing their goals. Much important assessment material is gathered, in particular concerning ideas of low frustration tolerance.

2.4   In-Vivo Therapy Sessions.   Sacco (1981) has outlined the value of conducting therapy sessions in real-life settings in which clients experience emotional difficulties. I have found moving outside the interview room to such settings particularly useful in gaining assessment material when traditional methods have failed to provide such data. For example, I once saw a male student who complained of avoiding social situations. He did so in case others would see his hands tremble. Traditional assessment methods yielded no further data.   To overcome this treatment impasse, I suggested to him that we needed to collect more data and we eventually conducted a therapy session in a coffee bar where I asked him to go and get us both a cup of coffee. He refused because he feared that his hands might tremble, but I firmly persisted with my request. He was able to identify a stream of negative cognitions on the way from our table to the service counter. He returned without our coffees but with valuable information which we processed later in my office. Again it is important for therapists to explain their rationale for conducting in-vivo sessions in advance in order to gain client cooperation.   In addition, obtaining clients' reactions to these sessions is often helpful particularly if in-vivo sessions are planned for use later in the therapeutic process.

SUMMARY

In this chapter, a rationale for the use of vivid methods in RET was presented. A number of methods were outlined to help therapists obtain important data at the assessment stage of therapy. These included imagery methods, the use of vivid, connotative therapist language, the use of photographs and other momentoes and the 'interpersonal nightmare technique' - all of which are designed to vividly portray activating events for clients. Furthermore, the use of (1) rational-emotive problem solving methods, (2) dreams, and (3) in-vivo therapy sessions were discussed.

It was stressed that the use of such methods can sometimes be risky and may on occasion threaten the therapeutic alliance.   To offset this risk, therapists whenever possible would be wise to disclose to clients the rationale for the use of such methods and elicit client cooperation. Furthermore it is important to gain clients' reactions to these methods afterwards.   However, since such methods quite often help therapists and clients overcome obstacles to assessment and move therapy forwards, it was argued that such risks that exist are well worth taking.

Chapter Five

VIVID RET II: DISPUTING METHODS

In this chapter, various vivid disputing
methods will be outlined. The purpose of these
methods is to (1) help clients see the untenable
basis and dysfunctional nature of their irrational
beliefs and to replace them with more rational ones
and (2) help them make more accurate inferences
about reality. These methods often demonstrate the
rational message powerfully but indirectly and they
do not necessarily call upon the client to answer
such questions as "where is the evidence . . . ?"
It is important for the therapist to make
certain preparations before initiating vivid disputing methods since the success of such methods
depends upon (1) the client clearly understanding
the link between thoughts, feelings and behaviours
and (2) the therapist discovering certain biographical information about the client.

1.   PREPARING FOR VIVID DISPUTING

1.1 Thought-Feeling-Behaviour link.   After
the therapist has undertaken a thorough assessment
of the client's target problem, her next task is to
help the client see the connection between thoughts,
feelings and behaviour. Here, again, vivid methods
can be employed. Thus the therapist, while speaking
with the client, might pick up a book and drop it to
the ground and continue talking to the client.
After a while, if the client has made no comment,
the therapist can ask him for both his affective and
cognitive reactions to this incident. Thus, the
client is given a vivid 'here and now' example of
the thought-feeling link.
1.2 Biographical   Information.   Before
initiating the vivid disputing process I often find

it helpful to gather certain information about the client.

(a) I often find it helpful to find out about my client's interests, hobbies and work situation. I have found that this information often helps me adapt my interventions, using phrases that will be meaningful to my client given his idiosyncratic life situation. Thus, if my client is passionately interested in boxing, a message utilising a boxing analogy may well have greater impact on him than a golfing analogy.

(b) I also find it helpful to discover who are the people that my client admires. I do this, for later, I may wish to ask my client how he thinks these admired individuals might solve similar problems. This prompts the client to identify with a model whom he can imitate. Lazarus (1978) has employed a similar method with children. For example, I asked a male client to imagine that his admired grandfather experienced public speaking anxiety and enquired how he would have overcome it. This helped him identify a coping strategy which he used to overcome his own public speaking anxiety problem. This approach is best used if the client can also acknowledge that the admired individual is also fallible and thus prone to human irrationality. It is important that the client also sees the feasibility of imitating the model.

(c) I find it invaluable to ask my clients about their previous experiences of attitude change. I try and discern the salient features of such change for possible replication in my in-session disputing strategies. For example, one anxious female client told me she had changed her mind about fox-hunting after reading a number of personal accounts in which arguments against fox-hunting were put. As part of my disputing plan, I directed this client to autobiographies of people who had overcome anxiety. Another client claimed that she had in the past experienced help from speaking to people who had experienced problems similar to her own. I arranged for this client to speak to some of my ex-clients who had experienced but overcome similar problems.

I now propose to outline a number of ways in which rational-emotive therapists can vividly employ disputing techniques. The importance of tailoring interventions to meet the specific, idiosyncratic requirements of clients should be borne in mind throughout.

2.   VIVID DISPUTING METHODS

2.1 Disputing in the Presence of Vivid Stimuli. In chapter one, I outlined a number of ways of vividly portraying activating events to help clients identify their emotional reactions and the cognitive determinants of these reactions. I outlined various visual, language, auditory and olfactory methods. These same methods can be used as context material in the disputing process. For example, one client brought along a drawing of herself and her mother. She portrayed her mother as a very large, menacing figure, and herself as a small figure crouching in fear in front of her mother. I asked the client to draw another picture where she and her mother were of the same height standing face-to-face looking each other in the eye. When she brought in this drawing, I enquired how her attitude towards her mother differed in the two drawings. This not only provided her with a demonstration that it was possible for her to evaluate her mother differently but also led to a fruitful discussion in which I disputed some of her irrational beliefs which were inherent in the first drawing, while having her focus on the second. A similar tactic was employed using the 'interpersonal nightmare technique' with a 55 year-old woman (see chapter four for the scenario). After disputing some of the irrational beliefs which were uncovered when the technique was employed for assessment purposes, I repeatedly played the woman the tape while having her dispute some of the ir-rational beliefs which listening to the tape un-covered. A similar method can be used when in-vivo sessions are conducted. In chapter four, I reported the case of a student who was anxious lest his hands should shake in public. Both assessment and later disputing of his irrational beliefs were carried out in a coffee bar. Indeed he practiced disputing his irrational beliefs while carrying two shaking cups of coffee back from the service counter to our table. Disputing in the presence of vivid stimuli enables the client to build bridges from in-session to out of session situations.

2.2 Imagery Methods. One very effective imagery method that can be used in the disputing of irrational beliefs is that of time projection (Lazarus, 1978). When clients make grossly exaggerated negative evaluations of an event, they often stop thinking about it and therefore cannot see beyond its "dreaded" implications. The purpose of time projection is to enable clients to vividly see that time and the world continue after the "dreaded event" has occurred. Thus, for example, a Malaysian student whose tuition fees were paid for by his village concluded that it would be terrible if he failed his exams because he couldn't bear to face his fellow villagers. I helped him to imagine his return to his village while experiencing shame. I then gradually advanced time forward in imagery. He began to see that it was likely that his fellow villagers would eventually come to adopt a compassionate viewpoint towards him, and even if they did not, he could always live happily in another part of the country or in another part of the world.

Imagery methods which focus on helping clients think more carefully and critically about "dreaded" events are also extremely valuable. For example, another client who had a fear of other people seeing his hands shake, was asked to imagine going into a bar, ordering a drink and drinking while his hands shook. He said that he would be extremely anxious about this because other people in the bar would stare at him. He was asked to imagine how many people would stare at him. Would they stare in unison or would they stare one at a time? He was asked to imagine how often they would stare at him, how long they would stare at him, and how often in the evening they would resume staring at him. He concluded that everybody would not stare at him and those who did stare would possibly only stare for about 30 seconds and he could stand that. This and other methods illustrate that it is possible to simultaneously help clients dispute both their faulty inferences and irrational evaluations. Another technique I employed with this same client was "imagery to exaggeration". He was asked to imagine his hands shaking while consuming drink and with everybody in the bar staring at him continually for three hours. At this point he burst out laughing and realised the exaggerated nature of his inference.

Rational-emotive imagery is a frequently employed technique and has been fully described by Maultsby and Ellis (1974) and Ellis (1979e). It often has dramatic impact and thus qualifies as a vivid method. It is worthwhile noting at this point that some clients have difficulty conjuring up images and may have to be trained in a stepwise fashion to utilise this ability. Furthermore, while helpful, it is probably not necessary for clients to imagine scenes with extreme clarity.

2.3 <u>The Rational-Emotive Therapist as Raconteur</u>. Wessler and Wessler (1980) have outlined the therapeutic value of relating various stories, parables, witty sayings, poems, aphorisms, and jokes to clients. The important factor here is that the therapist modifies the content of these to fit the client's idiosyncratic situation. Telling identical stories to two different clients may well have two different effects. One client may be deeply affected by the story, while for another the story may prove meaningless. It is important that rational-emotive therapists become acquainted with a wide variety of these stories, etc. and be prepared to modify them from client to client without introducing unwarranted distortions.

2.4 <u>Active-Visual Methods</u>. Active-visual methods combine therapist or client activity with a vivid visual presentation. Young (1980) has outlined one such method which he uses to help clients see the impossibility of assigning a global rating to themselves. He asks a client to describe some of his behaviours, attributes, talents, interests, etc. With every answer that the client gives, Young writes the attribute etc. on a white sticky label and sticks the label on the client. This continues until the client is covered with white sticky labels and can begin to see the impossibility of assigning one global rating to such a complex being. Wessler and Wessler (1980) outline similar active-visual methods to communicate a similar point. For example, they ask their clients to assign a comprehensive rating to a basket of fruit or a desk. Clients are encouraged to actively explore the components of the fruit basket or desk, while attempting to assign a global rating to it.

2.5 <u>Visual Models</u>. I have previously described the use of visual models that I have devised, each of which demonstrates a rational message (Dryden, 1980b). For example, I employ a model called the "LFT Splash". In the model, a young man is seated at the top of a roller-coaster with a young woman standing at the bottom. I tell clients that the young man does not move because he is telling himself that he can't stand the splash. Clients are asked to think what the young man would have to tell himself in order to reach the pretty girl. This model is particularly useful in introducing to clients the idea of tolerating acute time-limited discomfort which, if tolerated, would help them achieve their goals.

2.6 <u>Flamboyant Therapist Actions</u>. A common disputing strategy that rational-emotive therapists use in verbal dialogue, when clients conclude they are stupid for acting stupidly, is to ask some variant of the question "How are you a stupid person for acting stupidly?" Alternatively, instead of asking such questions, the therapist could suddenly leap to the floor and start barking like a dog for about 30 seconds and then resume his seat. He can then ask the client to evaluate his action. Clients usually say that the action is stupid. The therapist can then ask whether that stupid action makes him a stupid person. Such flamboyant actions often enable clients to more easily discriminate between global self-ratings and ratings of behaviours or attributes.

2.7 <u>Rational Role Reversal</u>. Rational role reversal has been described by Kassinove and DiGiuseppe (1975). In this technique, the therapist plays a naive client with an emotional problem that is usually similar to the client's. The client is encouraged to adopt the role of the rational-emotive therapist and help the 'client' dispute his irrational belief. As Kassinove and DiGiuseppe point out, this technique is best used after the client has developed some skill at disputing some of his own irrational ideas. A related technique has been devised by Burns (1980) which he calls 'externalization of voices'. In this technique, which is again used after the client has displayed some skill at disputing irrational beliefs, the therapist adopts the irrational part of the client's personality and supplies the client with irrational messages. The client's task is to repond rationally to the irrational messages. When clients show a high level of skill at this, the therapist, in role, can try hard to overwhelm the client with a barrage of quick-fire irrational messages thus helping the client to develop an automatic ability to respond to his own irrational messages. This method can also be used to help clients identify those negative thoughts to which they experience difficulty in responding.

2.8 <u>Therapist Self-Disclosure</u>. Some clients find therapist self-disclosure an extremely persuasive method while for others it is contra-indicated. One way of attempting to ascertain a client's possible reactions to therapist self-disclosure is to include an appropriate item in a pre-therapy questionnaire. It may well be wise to avoid using therapist self-disclosure with clients who respond negatively to the item. In any case, the therapist had better ascertain the client's reaction to any self-disclosing statements he might make. The research literature on this topic indicates that therapists had better not disclose personal information about themselves too early in the therapeutic process (Dies, 1973). When therapists do disclose information about themselves it is my experience that the most effective forms of self-disclosure are those in which the therapist portrays himself as a coping rather than a mastery model. Thus, for example, it is better for the therapist to say to the client: "I used to have a similar problem, but this is how I overcame it" rather than to say: "I have never had this problem, because I believe . . . "

2.9 <u>Paradoxical Therapist Actions</u>. This method is often best used when the client through his actions communicates a message about himself to the therapist which is based on irrational beliefs. For example, I once saw a female client who experienced a lot of rheumatic pain but had an attitude of low frustration tolerance towards it. Her behaviour towards me in sessions indicated the attitude: "I am a poor soul, feel sorry for me". This prompted me to adopt an overly sympathetic and diligent stance towards her. Thus, at the beginning of every session I treated her as if she could hardly walk and escorted her by arm to her chair and made frequent enquiries about her comfort. This eventually prompted her to make statements like: "Don't treat me like a child", "I can cope", "It's not as bad as all that", etc. I then helped her to identify and dispute some of the original implicit irrational messages. Whenever she began to lapse back into her self-pitying attitude, I began to behave in an overly solicitous manner again which provided a timely reminder for her to attend to the behavioural components of her philosophy of low frustration tolerance and thence to the philosophy itself.

2.10 <u>Paradoxical Therapist Communications</u>. Ellis (1977e) has written on the use of humour in RET where the therapist humourously exaggerates clients' irrational beliefs. He points out the importance of using humour against the irrational belief, rather than as an ad hominem attack. Taking clients beliefs and inferences to an absurd conclusion is another paradoxical technique that

can be used. Thus, for example, with clients who
are scared that other people may discover one of
their "shameful" acts or traits, therapists can take
this to its illogical conclusion by saying: "Well
there is no doubt about it, they will find out, then
they will tell their friends, some of whom will ring
up the local television station, and before you know
it you will be on the six o' clock news". Again it
is important that clients perceive that such
communications are being directed against their
beliefs rather than against them. Thus, feedback
from clients on this matter had better be sought.

2.11 <u>Rational Songs</u>. Ellis (1977e) has
written about the use of his, now famous, rational
songs in therapy. For example, the therapist can
hand a client a song sheet and sing, preferably in
an outrageous voice, a rational song which has been
carefully selected to communicate the rational
alternatives to the client's target irrational
belief. Since Ellis tends to favour songs that have
been written many years ago, it may be more
productive for the therapist to re-write the words
to more up-to-date and popular songs for clients not
familiar with some of the "old favourites".

2.12 <u>In-Session Inference Tests</u>. Clients are
likely to make similar faulty inferences about their
therapist to those they make about other people in
their own lives. For example, one of my clients saw
me talking to a fellow therapist at the end of one
of our sessions. At our next session she told me
that she was anxious about this because she was
convinced that I had been talking about her and
laughing about what she had told me in the session
(she was not in fact paranoid). I proceeded to pull
out two pieces of paper, kept one for my self and
gave the other one to her. I told her that I wanted
to find out whether she indeed had extraordinary
mind-reading powers. I thus wrote down the word
"chicken" on my piece of paper and asked her to
concentrate very carefully for the next three
minutes and to write down what she thought I was
thinking about. I said that I would keep thinking
about the word I had written down to make it a fair
experiment. After the three minutes, she wrote down
the word "baseball". This became known as the
"baseball-chicken" interview which she recalled
frequently when she made arbitrary inferences
concerning the meaning of other peoples' behaviour.

2.13 <u>Using the Therapist-Client Relationship</u>.
Wessler (1982a) has written that it is important for
the rational-emotive therapist to enquire about the

nature of his client's reactions to him i.e. to examine some of the client's here and now attitudes. Little has been written about this approach in the rational-emotive literature and thus relatively little is known about its potential as a framework for disputing inaccurate inferences and irrational beliefs. Wessler (1982a) also advocates that the therapist gives the client frank feedback about his impact on him and to explore whether the client has a similar impact on other people. Such generalisations must of course be made with caution but such discussion is often a stimulus for clients to become more sensitive to their impact on other people and often leads them to ask other people about their interpersonal impact (Anchin and Kiesler, 1982).

The advantage of using the therapist-client relationship in this way is that it provides both parties with an opportunity to process the client's inferences and beliefs in an immediate and often vivid fashion. The outcome of such strategies is often more memorable for clients than the outcome of more traditional disputing methods where client inferences and beliefs about recent past events are processed.

2.14 <u>Therapist   Paralinguistic/Nonverbal Behaviour</u>. When rational-emotive therapists want to emphasize a point, one important way of doing so is for them to vary their paralinguistic and non-verbal behaviour. For example, Walen et al. (1980) note that when Ellis in his public demonstrations talks about something being 'awful' he "drops his voice several notes, stretches out the word and increases his volume, producing a dreary and dramatic sound" for example "and it's AWWWWWFULL that he doesn't like me". Later when he changes the word 'awful' to 'unfortunate' or a 'need' to a 'want' Ellis again pronounces the words now reflecting rational concepts in a distinct way. He speaks the key word slowly, enunciates very clearly and raises the pitch of his voice as well as the volume" (page 178). In addition, the therapist might associate some dramatic non-verbal behaviour with the paralinguistic clue. For example, when the word "awful" is pronounced, the therapist might sink to the floor, holding his neck as if strangling himself.

2.15 <u>Therapeutic Markers</u>. Another way of emphasizing a point is to draw the client's attention to the fact that an important point is about to be made. For example, I might say to a

client when I want to emphasize a point "Now I want
you to listen extremely carefully to this point
because if you miss it it would be awwwfull"
(Therapist sinks to the floor again).   I call such
interventions "therapeutic markers".   Another way
of emphasizing statements is to change one's body
position.   For example, by moving his body trunk
forward towards the client, the therapist can
indicate the importance of his following statement.
Whenever I want clients to become aware of important
statements that they have made, particularly when
they make more rational statements at the beginning
of the disputing process, I may for example pause
and say: "Excuse me, could you just repeat what you
said, I really want to make a note of this".   If I am
recording a session, I might say: "Hold on a
minute, I really want you to hear what you have just
said, I can't believe it myself, I just want to
check it out".   I then replay them the relevant
portion of the tape.

2.16 <u>Pragmatic Disputes</u>.   One major way of
encouraging clients to surrender their irrational
beliefs in favour of more rational ones, is to point
out to them, and in this context in dramatic terms,
the implications of continued adherence to their
irrational beliefs.   Ellis counsels that for
particularly resistant and difficult clients this
tactic is often the most effective (Ellis, 1982,
personal communication).   Quite often I have heard
Ellis tell clients something like: "If you continue
to cling to that belief you'll suffer for the rest
of your life".   Here, as before, he changes his
paralinguistic and nonverbal behaviour when he
states the conclusion: "You'll suffer for the rest
of your life".   In a similar vein, when clients
state that they can't (or rather won't) change their
beliefs, he points out to them the logical
implications of not doing so when he says forcefully: "So, suffer!".   In this regard it would be
interesting to determine under what conditions
pragmatic disputes are more effective than
philosophical ones.

<u>SUMMARY</u>

In this chapter, I have outlined a variety of
ways in which therapists can make the disputing
process more vivid and memorable for clients.   I
underlined that tailoring interventions to fit
clients' idiosyncracies is most important and
suggested ways of doing this.   The point was made

that what might work for one client may very well
not work for another.   In conclusion, I would
encourage therapists to adopt an experimental
attitude towards their interventions and to
continually monitor the effect of their interventions by requesting feedback from clients as Beck
et al. (1979) advocate. This would help therapists
to construct, for each client, a profile of the
types of disputing tactics that are effective and
the types that prove ineffective.

Chapter Six

VIVID RET III: THE WORKING THROUGH PROCESS

This chapter focuses on how therapists can help clients to vividly work through some of their emotional problems. Ellis (1983b) has criticised some popular behavioural techniques on the grounds that they do not necessarily encourage clients to make profound philosophical changes in their lives. In particular, he identifies those behavioural techniques which encourage the client to go gradually as techniques which may indeed reinforce some clients' low frustration tolerance ideas. Whenever possible then, rational-emotive therapists try and encourage their clients to act in dramatic and vivid ways because they consider that significant attitude change is more likely to follow the successful completion of such tasks. In this chapter, I will outline the vivid methods that clients can put into practice behaviourally and cognitively in their everyday lives. However, rational-emotive therapists face a further problem which has received insufficient attention in the RET literature: namely how to encourage clients to remember to carry out their homework assignments.

1.   VIVID CUES FOR ENCOURAGING CLIENTS TO INITIATE THE WORKING THROUGH PROCESS

While some clients conscientiously put into practice homework assignments that they and their therapists have negotiated, other clients do not. While it is true that some clients do not follow through on homework assignments because of low frustration tolerance ideas, I have discovered that other clients do not do so, particularly early on in the working through process, because they require some vivid reminders to initiate this process. With such clients, I have found it particularly helpful to ask them what they generally find memorable in everyday life experiences. For example, some people find the printed word memorable while others have visual images which they remember. Yet others find stimuli in the auditory channel memorable. I often find that it is profitable for me to capitalise on whatever channel the client finds most memorable.

1.1 Vivid Visual Cues. There are a number of ways that clients can remind themselves to initiate the disputing process. A number of rational-emotive therapists encourage clients to carry around small 3" x 5" cards with rational self-statements written on them to which clients can refer at various times. Other therapists have encouraged clients to write reminders to themselves either to initiate a home-work assignment or to refer to a rational message. These clients are encouraged to pin up such messages at various places around the home or in their work situation.

I find it helpful to encourage those clients who find visual images particularly memorable to associate a particular dysfunctional feeling with a visual image which would enable them to initiate the disputing process. Thus one client found it particularly helpful to conjure up a sign in her mind which said: "Dispute". She would do so at times when she began to feel anxious. Another client, who was depressed, began to associate the onset of depression with a road sign on which was written: "Act now".

Another strategy I have used is to ascertain from clients what, if any, in-session experiences they have found particularly memorable. I try to help them encapsulate some of these experiences as a cue either to initiate the disputing process or to remind themselves of the relevant rational principle to which this experience referred. One client who was prone to thinking of himself as an idiot for acting idiotically, found an occasion when I pulled strange faces at him particularly memorable in helping him to get the point that concluding that he was an idiot for acting idiotically was an overgeneralisation. Whenever he began to make such an overgeneralisation in his everyday life, he would get the image of my pulling faces and quickly remember what this referred to. This helped him to accept himself for any idiotic act that he actually made or think that he might make in the future.

Another client who was extremely passive in therapy and, for a while, did virtually no cognitive disputing nor behavioural assignments outside the

session was helped in the following manner.   First
of all, this issue was made the focus of therapy.
Instead   of   asking   her   traditional   disputing
questions, I asked her to imagine what I would say
to her were I to respond to her irrational beliefs.
She   in   fact   had   understood   rational   principles
because her answers were very good.   Her problem was
that   she   would   not   employ   these   principles.
However, I asked her whether there was any way that
she   could   conjure   up   a   picture   of   me   giving   her
rational messages at various emotionally vulnerable
times in her everyday life.   She hit on the idea of
imagining   that   I   was   perched   on   her   shoulder
whispering   rational   messages   in   her   ear.
Furthermore she began to carry around a small card
which said on it: "Imagine that Dr Dryden is on
your   shoulder".   This   proved   a   particularly
effective technique where all else had failed.
        1.2   Vivid Language.   Wexler and Butler (1976)
have argued in favour of therapists using expressive
language in therapy.   I have found that one of the
major   benefits   of   my   using   vivid   non-profane
language   in   therapy   is   that   clients   remember
particular vivid expressions or catch-phrases and
use these as shorthand ways of disputing irrational
beliefs in their everyday lives.   For example, in
chapter five, I mentioned a case where I helped a
client to dispute a particular distorted inference
by having her attempt to read my mind.   I wrote down
the word "chicken" on a piece of paper and asked her
to guess what I had written.   She in fact wrote down
the word "baseball".   I suggested that we call this
particular   interview   the   "baseball-chicken"
interview.   She   found   this   quite   memorable   and
whenever she began thinking that other people were
making   negative   inferences   about   her   without
supporting   data,   she   would   remember   the   phrase
"baseball and chicken".   This served (1) as a
timely   reminder   that   she   may   be   making   incorrect
conclusions from the data at hand, and (2) as a cue
for her to start examining the evidence.
        In a related technique, the therapist asks the
client to give his own distinctive name to a faulty
psychological process.   Wessler and Wessler (1980)
give such an example where a client came to refer to
himself as "Robert the Rulemaker" to describe his
tendency   to   make   demands   on   himself   and   other
people.   A knowledge of clients' sub-cultural values
is particularly helpful here.   I work in a working
class area in Birmingham, England, and one word that
my clients frequently used, which was unfamiliar to

me, was the word 'mather'[1].   I helped one client who
had an anger problem towards her mother, to see that
her mother was a fallible human being with a worrying problem and could be accepted for this rather
than be damned for it.   My client suddenly laughed
and said "Yes, I guess my mother is a matherer".   I
encouraged her to remember this catchy phrase whenever she began to feel angry towards her mother.

Ellis   (personal   communication)   often
deliberately uses obscene or scatalogical language
with clients to help "open them up and get at their
personal problems in a more rapid and effective
manner" than achieved with blander language.   He
also encourages clients to use such language with
themselves to make disputing a more forceful and
vivid experience. (Ellis, 1979c).   However, as with
other techniques, obscene therapist language may
well backfire with some clients.

1.3 Auditory   Cues.   Rational-emotive
therapists usually make it a practice to encourage
clients to make tape recordings of their sessions to
replay several times between sessions.   This often
serves to remind clients of rational principles that
they have understood in the session but may have
forgotten between sessions.   With the advent of
cheap personal stereo systems, clients can usually
listen to the tape recordings of their sessions at
varioius times of the day.   Again using personal
stereo systems, clients can be encouraged to develop
auditory reminders to initiate either cognitive or
behavioural homework assignments.   In addition,
they can be encouraged to put forceful and emphatic
rational statements on cassettes and play these
while undertaking behavioural assignments.   For
example, I once saw a client who was anxious about
other people looking at her because she was scared
that they might think her strange.   I suggested that
she do something in her everyday life which would
encourage people to look at her so that she could
dispute some of the underlying irrational beliefs.
She decided to wear a personal stereo system in the
street which she thought would encourage people to
look at her.   I suggested that while walking she
play a tape on which she had recorded the rational
message: "Just because I look strange doesn't mean
that I am strange".

The use of rational songs in therapy has
already been described in chapter five and by Ellis
(1977e).   Several of my clients have found that
singing a particular rational song at an emotionally
vulnerable time has been helpful for them.   It has

reminded them of a rational message that they might not ordinarily have been able to focus on while being emotionally distressed.   Another client told me that her sessions with me reminded her of a particular song and whenever she hummed this song to herself it helped bring to mind the fact that she could accept herself even though she did not have a man in her life.   The song ironically was "You're no-one till somebody loves you".   In fact she re-wrote some of the words and changed the title to "You're someone even though nobody loves you".

   1.4 <u>Olfactory Cues</u>.   It is possible for clients to use various aromas as cues to remind themselves to do a homework assignment or to initiate the disputing process for themselves.   One client said that she found my pipe tobacco particularly aromatic and distinctive.   Since we were both seeking a memorable cue, I suggested an experiment whereby she purchased a packet of my favourite tobacco and carried this around with her to smell at various distressing times.   This aroma was associated in her mind with a particular rational message.   This proved helpful and indeed my client claimed that by saying to herself the phrase: "Pipe up", she now no longer has to take the tobacco out of her handbag to smell.   Just the phrase "pipe up" is enough to remind her of the rational message.

2.   THE WORKING THROUGH PROCESS

   From its inception, RET has strongly recom-mended that a client undertakes "some kind of activity which itself will act as a forceful counter propagandist agency against the nonsense he believes" (Ellis, 1958).   Ellis has consistently stressed that for clients who will agree to do them, dramatic, forceful, and implosive activities remain the best forms of working through assignments (Ellis, 1979c).   Such assignments emphasize either cognitively-based or behavioural activities.

   2.1 <u>Cognitive Assignments</u>.   In cognitive assignments, clients are encouraged to find ways in which they can convince themselves (outside therapy sessions) that rational philosophies which they can acknowledge as correct in therapy sessions are indeed correct and functional for them.   Ellis has always urged clients to dispute their ideas vigorously using such aids as written homework forms or 'disputing irrational belief' forms (DIBS) (Ellis, 1979e).   Other vivid cognitive techniques that clients can use include the following:

Vivid RET III: The Working Through Process

(a) <u>Rational Proselytizing</u> (Bard, 1973). Here clients are encouraged to teach RET to their friends. In teaching others, clients become more convinced themselves of rational philosophies. This technique, however, had better be used with caution and clients warned against playing the role of unwanted therapist to friends and relatives.

(b) <u>Tape-recorded Disputing</u>. In this technique, clients are encouraged to put on tape a disputing sequence. They are asked to play both the rational and irrational part of themselves. Clients are further encouraged to try and make the rational part of themselves more persuasive and more forceful in responding to the irrational part of themselves.

(c) For those clients who are intellectually unable to do cognitive disputing in its classical sense, the use of <u>passionate rational self-statements</u> can be advocated. Here client and therapist work together to develop appropriate rational self-statements which the client can actually use in his everyday life. Clients are encouraged to repeat these statements to themselves in a passionate and forceful manner instead of in their normal voice tone. Another variation of this technique is to have clients say rational self-statements to their reflection in a mirror using a passionate tone and dramatic gestures to again reinforce the message.

(d) Other techniques which my clients have used which relate to the same theme include the writing of modern rational songs, rational short stories and rational poetry.

2.2 <u>Behavioural Techniques</u>. Behavioural techniques which rational-emotive therapists particularly favour involve clients doing cognitive disputing in settings which vividly evoke their fears. The purpose is to enable clients to have the success experience of doing cognitive disputing while exposing themselves to feared stimuli in the physical or social environment. In addition, dramatic, behavioural assignments are recommended to help clients overcome their low frustration tolerance ideas. Here the focus is oriented towards clients changing their dysfunctional attitudes towards their internal experiences of anxiety, frustration, etc.

Rational-emotive therapists have encouraged their clients to do the following kinds of vivid and dramatic assignments.

(a) <u>Shame-Attacking Exercises</u>. Here the client is encouraged to do some act which he has previously regarded as 'shameful'. He is encouraged

86

to act in a 'shameful' way which will encourage
other people in the environment to pay attention to
him without bringing harm to himself or other people
or without unduly alarming others.   The client is
encouraged to simultaneously engage in vigorous
disputing such as: "I may look weird, but I'm not
weird".   In my opinion, one of the drawbacks of
encouraging a client to do shame-attacking
exercises in groups is that the group in fact serves
to positively reinforce the client for doing the
exercise.   Clients often do shame-attacking
exercises together and again the drawback is that
the whole exercise becomes a game and something
which is not taken seriously.   However, in my
opinion, shame-attacking exercises are extremely
valuable in promoting change, and while humour is an
important component part, my experience is that
greater and longer lasting change is effected when
clients do shame-attacking exercises on their own as
part of their individual therapy without the social
support of a group.

      (b) Risk-Taking Assignments.   In risk-taking
assignments, clients are encouraged to do something
which they regard as being 'risky'.   For example, a
client may be encouraged to ask a waiter to replace
a set of cutlery because it is too dirty.   In
preparing clients for risk-taking exercises,
identification and disputing of faulty inferences
and consequent irrational evaluations needs to be
done.   The problem here, however, is to get the
client to encounter the 'dire' responses from others
that he predicts he will meet.   In order for
evaluative change to take place the client had
better be prepared to do such risk-taking experiences repeatedly over a long period of time so
that he eventually encounters the 'dire' response.
This is because such 'dire' responses from others
occur far less frequently than the client predicts.
Again the client is encouraged to undertake cognitive disputing along with the behavioural act.

      (c) Step-Out-of Character Exercises.   Wessler
(1982a) has developed this exercise modifying it
from Kelly's fixed-role therapy (Kelly, 1955).
Clients are encouraged to identify desired behavioural goals which are not currently enacted with
frequency.   These exercises may contain elements of
overcoming shame and taking risks but do not have
to.   Thus, for example, one group member chose the
goal of eating more slowly, which for him was a
desirable non-shameful, non-risky exercise, but one
which involved considerable monitoring of eating

habits and cognitive disputing of low frustration tolerance ideas.

(d)   <u>In-Vivo Desensitisation</u>.   These methods require clients to repeatedly confront their fears in an implosive manner.   For example, clients with elevator phobia are asked to ride in elevators twenty to thirty times a day right at the start of treatment instead of gradually working their way up to this situation either in imagery or in actuality. Again simultaneous cognitive disputing is urged. Neuman (1982) has written on and presented tapes of short-term group-oriented treatment of phobias.   In this group, clients are encouraged to rate their levels of anxiety.   The most important goal is for clients to experience a 'level 10' which is extreme panic.   Neuman continually points out to people that it is important to experience 'level 10' because only then can they learn that they can survive and live through such an experience.   Similarly, it is important for rational-emotive therapists to work toward helping clients to tolerate extreme forms of anxiety before helping clients to reduce this anxiety, if inroads to severe phobic conditions are to be made.

(e)   <u>Stay-in-There Activities</u>.   Grieger and Boyd (1980) have described a similar technique which they call "stay-in-there" activities, the purpose of which is to have clients vividly experience that they can tolerate and put up with uncomfortable experiences.   One of my clients wanted to overcome her car driving phobia.   One of the things she feared was that her car would stall at a set of traffic lights and she would be exposed to the wrath of motorists who were stuck behind her.   After illiciting and disputing her irrational ideas in traditional verbal dialogue, I encouraged her to actually turn off her engine at a set of lights and to stay there for about twenty minutes, thus creating the impression that her car had broken down.   Fortunately, the other car drivers did react in an angry fashion and she was able to practice disputing her dire needs for approval and comfort in a situation in which she remained for fully half an hour.

Some clients tend to do these dramatic exercises once or twice and then drop them from their repertoire.   Therapists are often so glad and so surprised that their clients will actually do these assignments that they do not consistently show their clients the importance of <u>continuing</u> to do these dramatic assignments.   One of the reasons for continued practice has already been mentioned, namely that clients are more likely to make inferential changes than evaluative changes by doing these assignments infrequently. This is largely because the 'dreaded' event has a far lower probability of occurring than clients think. However, sooner or later, if clients consistently and persistently put into practice the above assignments they may well encounter such events which will provide a context for disputing of irrational beliefs. Thus, if therapists really want to encourage clients to make changes at 'B' as well as at 'A', they had better be prepared to consistently encourage clients to do these dramatic assignments over a long period of time.

2.3 <u>Reward and Penalty Methods</u>. Ellis (1979e) has consistently employed reward-penalty methods to encourage clients to take responsibility for being their own primary agent of change. Here clients are encouraged to identify and employ positive reinforcements for undertaking working through assignments and penalties when they do not do so. While not all clients require such encouragement, difficult and resistant clients, whose resistance is due to low frustration tolerance ideas, can be encouraged to take full responsibility for not putting into practice assignments that would stimulate change. Thus, dramatic experiences like burning a ten dollar bill, throwing away an eagerly awaited meal, cleaning a dirty room at the end of a hard day's work, are experiences which are designed to be so aversive that clients would choose to do the assignment that has previously been avoided rather than exacting the penalty. Of course clients can, and often do, refuse to do the assignment and refuse to employ reward-penalty methods. However, other clients who have been resistant in the working through process have, in my experience, began to move when the therapist adopts this no-nonsense approach.

3. <u>LIMITATIONS OF VIVID METHODS IN RET</u>

While the basic thesis in Chapters 4, 5 and 6 has been to show the possible efficacy of vivid RET, there are, of course, limitations of such an approach.

(a) It is important for therapists to determine the impact of introducing vivid methods into the therapeutic process with clients. Thus, using the guidelines of Beck et al. (1979), it is perhaps wise for the therapist to ask the client at various points in the therapeutic process to give frank feedback to the therapist concerning the therapist's methods and activities. While the therapist may not always agree not to use such techniques just because a client has a negative reaction to them, we had better obtain and understand our clients' negative reactions to our procedures.

(b) It is important in the use of vivid-dramatic techniques not to overload the client. One vivid and dramatic method carefully introduced into a therapy session at an appropriate time is much more likely to be effective than several dramatic methods employed indiscriminately in a session.

(c) It is important that rational-emotive therapists have the rationale for the use of such vivid methods clear in their minds and do not see the use of such methods as a goal in itself. The important thing to remember is that such vivid methods are to be used as a vehicle for promoting client attitude change and not to make the therapeutic process more stimulating for the therapist. It is also extremely important to ascertain what the client has learned from the vivid methods that the therapist has employed or urged him to employ. The client will not magically come to the conclusion that the therapist wants him to. It is also important that therapists do not promote 'false' change in their clients. Change is 'false' when the client feels better as a result of some of these vivid methods but does not get better. Ellis (1972) has written an important article on such a distinction. Thus therapists should invariably ask questions like: "What have you learned from doing this vivid method?" and "How can you strengthen this learning experience for yourself outside of therapy?"

(d) Dramatic and vivid methods are not appropriate for all clients. They are particularly helpful for those clients who use intellectualisation as a defence and/or who use verbal dialogue to tie rational-emotive therapists in knots. While there is no data at the moment to support the following hypothesis, I would speculate that dramatic and vivid methods had better not be used with clients who have an overly dramatic and hysterical personality. It is perhaps more appropriate to assist such clients to reflect in a calm and undramatic manner on their experiences than to overstimulate an already highly stimulated personality.

However, if therapists keep these and other problems in mind, it is my contention that the judicious use of vivid methods in RET can only enhance its effectiveness in effecting pervasive philosophical change in clients.

NOTE

1.   This is pronounced 'my-the' and means to be worried or bothered.

Chapter Seven

PAST MESSAGES AND DISPUTATIONS: THE CLIENT AND
SIGNIFICANT OTHERS

Rational-emotive therapy is a comprehensive
treatment approach which aims to deal with the three
basic modalities of human dysfunctioning - cognitive, emotive and behavioural. Indeed, its multimodal focus is what initially attracted me to RET.
However, with regard to another important dimension
in psychotherapy - time perspective - rational-emotive theory is less comprehensive in its recom-
mendations. In listening to many tapes of RET
practitioners and in participating in discussions
with Institute faculty, fellows and practicum
students, I have noted that the large majority claim
(at least within earshot of others!) to follow
Ellis' teachings with regard to time perspective:
     "The rational therapist for the most part
     ignores connections between the client's early
     history and his present disturbances. He does
     not believe that the client was made neurotic
     by his past experiences, but by his own un-
     realistic and over-demanding interpretations
     of these experiences."
     (Ellis, 1977f, p. 27).
Thus, when clients have wanted to discuss their
past experiences, they are generally instructed by
the therapist that the reason they are anxious,
depressed, angry or guilty now is because they are
right now re-indoctrinating themselves with the
beliefs they had acquired in the past. Broadly
speaking, this is a sound approach and leads the
focus of RET practice to be present-centered and
future-oriented. However, I am a little concerned
with the apparent absolutistic manner in which
people have interpreted Ellis in this regard and
believe that with some clients, therapeutic movement is delayed by the practitioner's strong
reluctance to consider past material. This

reluctance is also evident in the RET literature; as far as I am aware, only Dombrow (1973) has made a similar plea for working with past material in RET.

My first thesis is that, while I concur with Ellis' view that "for the most part" exploring connections between the client's earlier history and his present disturbance may not be particularly helpful, with some clients exploring past material can actually enhance therapeutic movement. My second thesis is that this can be effectively done by helping clients to dispute the irrationality implicit in the messages they received in the past from significant others. This has the additional effect of enabling clients to recognize and accept the fallibility of those who were assumed to be infallible or omnipotent. To put this in a theoretical perspective, clients are helped to dispute the irrational belief suggested by Hauck (1967): "the idea that beliefs held by respected authorities or society must be correct and therefore should not be questioned." (p. 2).

Interestingly enough, I believe that rational-emotive therapists are not loathe to help clients dispute the irrationality implicit in messages they are receiving from people in their lives at present and the messages they may receive from people in the future. Of course, this is not the major focus of therapeutic intervention, since the practitioner will then proceed to help clients to dispute the irrationality implicit in the messages they give themselves in response to the irrational messages received from others. Thus, the principle of disputing the irrationality in others' messages is not altogether foreign to RET practice, although it would be viewed as an inelegant solution. While not foreign to RET practice, this procedure has received little attention in the RET literature. Moreover, while at present we have very little research evidence showing the superior effectiveness of elegant over inelegant RET solutions, the possibility may exist that such inelegant solutions may enhance therapeutic movement in some clients and thus deserve consideration.

To illustrate the thesis that helping some clients dispute the irrationality implicit in messages received from people in the past may facilitate therapeutic movement, I will briefly discuss the case of 'Mary'. Mary is a very intelligent, 32 year old Irish girl whom I saw in a University Health Service setting. Mary had suffered from severe feelings of worthlessness for many years. She had previously received therapeutic help from a kindly Irish psychiatrist who "boosted her ego" temporarily. However, needless to say, such "progress" was short-lived. In the traditional manner, I attempted to show Mary that her depression stemmed from the strict demands she placed on herself and the resulting self-downing which accompanied her failures to live up to these demands. However, Mary seemed more interested in talking at length about the inhumane treatment she had received from her parents when she was younger -she was cruelly beaten, often for little reason and particularly when she made mistakes. My repeated and forceful attempts to guide her to the view that her present disturbance was caused by present self-indoctrination did not lead to therapeutic progress. However, movement did occur after I had worked with Mary for a short period of time, helping her to analyze and dispute the irrationality implicit in the messages she had received from her parents in the past. This, in my view, enabled her to become more receptive to the view that it was not the parents' messages of A which caused her disturbance at C, but her own interpretations of the messages at B with which she was now re-indoctrinating herself. Mary's response to my change of therapeutic attack was illuminating. She claimed that the occasions when we analyzed and disputed her parents' irrationality were helpful in that: 'I felt freed then to look at what I am doing to myself now.'

In conclusion, while I have pointed out the advantages of helping some clients to dispute the irrationality implicit in messages received from significant others, - (1) it may help initially resistant clients to later respond more favourably to present-centred/future-oriented RET; (2) it has educational value in teaching that significant others are not infallible and have their own irrational beliefs; and finally (3) it helps make RET even more multi-modal in approach - I want to emphasize some potential dangers. First, if not sensitively handled, the client may learn that A really does cause C. Thus, it is important to stress to clients that whatever irrational messages were communicated to them by significant others, they are still responsible for determining their own emotional disturbance by the communication of equally irrational messages to themselves. Second - and related to the first issue - clients may begin to severely blame significant others for causing

them their problems. This is not a problem if the
issue of blame is then handled in the traditional
RET manner. Finally, delving into the past may lead
the practitioner and his client into blind alleys
and encourage the former to collude with the
latter's attempts to avoid self-responsibility.

Nonetheless, if the above problems are
competently handled, it is my contention that the
strategy of helping the client to analyze and
dispute the irrationality in past (present and
future) significant others' messages does have its
place in RET practice with certain clients.

Chapter Eight

RATIONAL-EMOTIVE THERAPY AND ECLECTICISM

It is possible to adopt an eclectic stance in psychotherapy and still be guided by theory proposed by a particular therapeutic orientation. This is illustrated by considering the clinical practice of rational-emotive therapists. Such therapists may select from diverse sources, systems and styles but their selections are determined by rational-emotive theory and a consideration of patient characteristics.

Eclecticism has been defined as "consisting of that which has been selected from diverse sources, systems or styles" (American Heritage Dictionary of the English Language, 1971) and much has been recently written on eclectic approaches in psychotherapy (e.g. Dryden, 1980a; Garfield, 1980; Lazarus, 1976; and Shostrom, 1976). However, there have been few attempts to clarify the decisions that clinicians make in broadening their therapeutic repertoire by selecting from diverse sources systems and styles while still adhering to a particular therapeutic orientation. The aim of this paper is to show what guides rational-emotive therapists in such endeavours.

Rational-emotive theory states that much emotional disturbance stems from the faulty inferences and irrational evaluations that patients make in endeavouring to make sense of themselves, other people and the world (Wessler and Wessler, 1980). Examples of faulty inferences have been detailed by Beck et al. (1979) and include arbitrary inferences, overgeneralizations and selective abstractions. Irrational evaluations are based on a philosophy of demandingness which hinders patients from achieving their long-term goals and restricts their opportunities to live effectively and creatively in the world. The major task of rational-emotive therapists is to help patients correct their faulty inferences and to replace their demanding philosophy with a desiring philosophy, i.e. one which is characterised by wants, preferences and wishes. To achieve their basic task, rational-emotive therapists focus on cognitive, affective and behavioural factors and consequently RET has been described as a comprehensive system of psychotherapy (Ellis and Abrahms, 1978).

Rational-emotive therapists then are guided by a particular theory of emotional disturbance and personality change (Ellis, 1978) and thus can be contrasted with eclectic therapists who de-emphasize theory (e.g. Lazarus, 1976). Theory is considered important by rational-emotive therapists for a number of reasons. First, theory provides testable propositions for empirical study. Second, as Frank (1970) has shown theory helps therapists gain emotional support from others with similar views and thus helps sustain the therapist's morale. The third and most important reason is that theory helps guide therapists in their work, helps them correctly select particular therapeutic procedures and gives them a framework for determining the consequences of such procedures. Eysenck (1970) also stresses the need for theory in psychotherapy and warns that without a theoretical framework the practice of eclectic therapists would be characterised by "a mish-mash of theories, a huggermugger of procedures, a charivaria of therapies and a gallimaufry of activities having no proper rationale and incapable of being tested or evaluated" (p. 145).

THERAPEUTIC PRACTICE

In the execution of their major task - effecting cognitive change, rational-emotive therapists attempt to engage patients in a concrete and situationally-based exploration of their problems. To encourage concreteness, therapists tend to use an implicit ABCDE framework in exploring their patients' problems. Point 'A' in the framework represents an event or the patient's perceptions and inferences concerning that event. 'B' represents the patient's beliefs or evaluations about the phenomenal event, while 'C' stands for the emotional and behavioural consequences of the patient's belief. At point D the therapist's task is to help the patient challenge his faulty inferences and irrational evaluations and replace them with more realistic and rational cognitions which leads to emotional and behavioural change at point 'E'.

In practice rational-emotive therapists tend to start at point 'C'. The major goal here is to help patients to acknowledge their feelings (without dwelling on them) and to identify their actions. In doing so the therapist may very well use procedures derived from other therapeutic systems. For example, if a patient experiences difficulty in acknowledging feelings, the rational-emotive therapist might employ a gestalt awareness exercise or psychodramatic technique with the specific purpose at this stage of encouraging the patient to acknowledge feelings.

After helping the patient to correctly identify emotional and behavioural responses, the therapist shifts her attention to the context in which such responses arise (point A). Exploration at this point involves the therapist paying attention to the patient's description of the relevant context. The patient is helped to describe his perception of the relevant situation fairly briefly. The therapist tends not to dwell on those events and discourages the patient from presenting too many or problem-irrelevant contexts. The goal of the therapist is to aid the patient in adequately framing the problem so that she can assist in the identification and correction of presently held faulty inferences and beliefs. In practice the context tends to be either one that is anticipated or one of recent occurrence and thus RET tends to be a present and future-oriented therapy. Rational-emotive therapists tend not to focus on events that have occurred in the distant past since it is argued that such exploration does not aid the correction of presently-held faulty cognitions (Ellis, 1962). However, Dryden (1979) has found that in certain circumstances such exploration does assist the therapist in her dissuasion strategies with some patients. Thus understanding the likely origins of presently-held beliefs may motivate such patients to change such beliefs. The point at issue here is that the purpose of exploring such past events is to facilitate the disputing of <u>presently</u> held inferences and beliefs.

At point B in the ABCDE framework, the therapist's task is to help the patient identify the irrational evaluations that the latter employs in appraising the relevant context. Here the therapist is not limited to verbal interventions such as: "what are you saying to yourself?", that are often seen in therapy transcripts. In fact, in the author's experience a common answer to such questions is - "nothing". In addition to psychodrama (Nardi, 1979) and gestalt methods, various role-playing and imagery methods may be used as an aid to facilitate the discovery of irrational beliefs. Indeed client-centred procedures for some patients may be employed. Such patients find the less active-directive style implicit in such procedures helpful in exploring and discovering meanings and beliefs (DiLoreto, 1971). Rather than abandon RET for client-centred therapy, an eclectic rational-emotive therapist would vary her therapeutic style but not the theoretical underpinnings of her system.

Point D in the framework is also called the dissuasion process (Wessler and Wessler, 1980). In attempting to dissuade the patient, the therapist may use a wide variety of cognitive, imaginal, affective, and behavioural methods, and may suggest similar procedures for the patient to use between sessions as the latter strives to put into practice in his everyday life what he has learned in therapy (point E).

THEORY - INSPIRED GUIDELINES FOR CHOOSING APPROPRIATE THERAPEUTIC PROCEDURES

Thus far it has been argued that rational-emotive therapists may choose from a range of cognitive, experiential and behavioural methods to facilitate their basic task of working within the ABCDE framework. However rational-emotive therapists are mindful of possible negative effects of employing certain procedures and by no means would employ all available procedures. There are a number of issues that rational-emotive therapists have in mind when deciding whether or not to employ a particular therapeutic procedure.

(a) Helping patients get better rather than feel better. One basic aim of rational-emotive therapists is to promote long-term philosophically-based change as opposed to helping patients feel better in the short-term. Thus rational-emotive therapists may deliberately avoid being unduly warm

99

towards their patients and would be wary of employing cathartic methods. The hazard of undue therapist warmth is that it may lead to increased long-term dependence in patients who may then believe that they are worthwhile because the therapist is acting very warmly towards them. However if the therapist or other significant people act coldly towards the patient, he may then conclude that he is worthless. Thus, undue therapist warmth, although patients feel better when so exposed, tends to distract clients from dealing with the more difficult task of accepting themselves unconditionally (Ellis, 1977g). For this reason an intense relationship between therapist and patient is generally avoided. The therapist strives to establsh and maintain a working relationship with her patient and strives to accept the patient as a fallible human being without being unduly warm towards him.

Cathartic methods have the short-term value of encouraging relief of pent-up feeling, but in the long-term if not employed sparingly and briefly often encourage patients to practice their already well-ingrained irrational philosophies. For example, cathartic procedures which place emphasis on the ventilation of intense angry feelings (e.g. pounding a cushion) run the risk of encouraging processes of blaming which are according to rational-emotive theory a feature of the irrational philosophy underlying anger. Rational-emotive therapists might employ such procedures when they wish to help patients to acknowledge their feelings, but the patient would then be quickly encouraged to consider the philosophy underlying such feelings.

(b) <u>Self-esteem vs. self-acceptance.</u> In RET, self-esteem is defined as a form of global self-rating and is to be avoided since according to rational-emotive theory it has problematic long-term implications for patients. Procedures based on self-esteem notions encourage patients to define themselves as worthwhile or competent so long as they gain approval or succeed at valued tasks. They are thus prone to defining themselves as worthless and incompetent if they receive disapproval or fail at the same tasks. Furthermore, rational-emotive theory states that it is nonsensical to give humans global ratings since they are on-going, complex ever-changing organisms who defy such ratings. As an alternative, rational-emotive therapists not only endeavour to get patients to accept themselves as on-going, complex, ever-changing fallible human beings, but also encourage them to rate their traits, aspects, and behaviour but not their selves. Many procedures do not in fact discourage patients from making such global self-ratings. For example, many therapists give patients homework assignments which are designed to encourage the patient to succeed. Thus a patient who succeeds at approaching a woman at a discotheque may conclude that because he has been able to do this, perhaps he is not worthless after all. The implication would be that if he failed in his assignment then this would be a confirmation of his worthlessness. Rational-emotive therapists by contrast may at times encourage patients to deliberately go out and fail since such a failure experience presents them with opportunities to work on accepting themselves as fallible humans rather than sub-humans when they fail. In reality, rational-emotive therapists suggest both success and failure-oriented homework assignments to their patients.

(c) <u>Anger vs. Annoyance</u>. Rational-emotive theory clearly distinguishes between anger and annoyance. Annoyance results when something occurs which we view as a trespass on our personal conceptual domain, which we strongly dislike but which we refrain from demanding should not have happened. There is an absence of blaming of self, other or the world for the deed, i.e. the deed is rated but the perpetrator of the deed is accepted. In contrast anger stems from the jehovian demand that the trespass should not have occurred and the trespasser is damnable. Therapists from other persuasions often do not make such a clear distinction and thus the therapeutic procedures which they employ may encourage the full expression and ventilation of anger rather than annoyance. If this occurs then rational-emotive therapists would avoid using these procedures. As mentioned earlier, while the full expression and ventilation of anger helps the person feel better it often encourages adherence to a long-term and damaging anger-creating philosophy. In RET, procedures are used to help patients to fully acknowledge their anger but then they are encouraged to dispute the underlying anger-creating philosophy.

(d) <u>Desensitization vs. Implosion</u>. Rational-emotive therapists face a choice of two different approaches when the issue of suggesting homework assignments to patients arises. They can either suggest that patients gradually face their fears and overcome their problems in a slow stepwise fashion while minimizing discomfort (desensitization). Or they can suggest that patients take a risk and forcefully confront their fears and their problems whie tolerating discomfort (implosion). Rational-emotive therapists very definitely favour implosion-based assignments since they help patients overcome their "low frustration tolerence" (LFT) or "discomfort anxiety", constructs which, according to rational-emotive theory, play a central role in preventing change (Wessler, 1978; Ellis, 1979g). Consequently such therapists would avoid helping patients to gradually and painlessly overcome their problems because such procedures are viewed as encouraging patients to cling to their philosophy of LFT which actually decreases their chances of maintaining therapeutic improvement and increases the possibility of relapse (Ellis, 1979g).

Due to the somewhat unusual stance taken on the above issues rational-emotive therapy has proved rather difficult to combine with other methods derived from different theoretical origins. Garfield and Kurtz (1977) make a similar observation, noting in their study of 154 clinicians' eclectic views that RET was occasionally combined with learning theory-based approaches but was not combined with psychoanalytic, neo-analytic, Rogerian, humanistic or Sullivanian orientations.

THERAPEUTIC STYLE

Ellis (1976) speaking for rational-emotive theory argues that humans have great difficulty maintaining the changes that they make more easily in the short-term because of the strong biological basis to irrational thinking. Because of this difficulty, Ellis urges rational-emotive therapists to adopt an active-directive, forceful and persistent therapeutic style and also encourage their patients to be equally active, forceful and persistent with themselves. However, is such a style beneficial with a wide range of patients? Or should rational-emotive therapists vary their therapeutic style with different patients? If the latter is to be advised, what criteria should be employed to assist rational-emotive therapists in these important decisions?

The first question remains unanswered since we lack research which has systematically studied the effects of active-directive RET across a wide range of patients. There is however some research evidence concerning different therapeutic styles with different patients which has relevance for RET practitioners. DiLoreto (1971) in a study using socially anxious patients found that active-directive RET was more effective with introverts than extroverts in the sample while client-centred therapy was more effective with extroverts. This suggests that RET practitioners might effectively adopt a less directive more reflective style of RET, when working with socially anxious extroverts. Morley and Watkins (1974) carried out a treatment study with speech anxious patients. They found that active-directive RET benefitted external locus of control patients most, while internal locus of control patients profited most from a modified RET approach where rational and irrational beliefs relevant to speech anxiety were merely presented and not challenged in the usual fashion. To what extent these findings can be generalized to other patient populations remains unclear. We must also wait for studies to consider Ellis' point often made in practica that the stronger patients adhere to irrational philosophies the more forceful the therapist had better be.

Carson (1969) advocates an interpersonally-based system to help the therapist vary her inter-personal style according to the patient's own style. Unproductive interlocking interactional patterns arise when the therapist adopts a manner of relating which confirms the patient in his own self-defeating style. The therapist's task is to adopt an inter-personal style which (a) does not reinforce the patient's dysfunctional style and (b) provides a disconfirming experience for the patient. For example, with a passive patient it would be important for the rational-emotive therapist to refrain from adopting a very active style which might reinforce the patient's self-defeating passivity.

Thus, rational-emotive therapists had better be mindful of Eschenroeder's (1979) question: "Which therapeutic style is most effective with what kind of client?" (p. 5).

THERAPEUTIC MODALITIES

Rational-emotive theory holds that the important modalities of human experience – cognitive (verbal and imaginal), affective and behavioural are overlapping rather than separate systems (Ellis, 1962). However it may be important for RET practitioners to vary the emphasis they place in working within the various modalities with different patients. What criteria might be important as guides to decision-making in this area bearing in mind that the ultimate goal is a common one (i.e. to effect philosophical changes)? One set of criteria might be the ability of patients to handle verbal concepts. The author's own experience of working as a counselling psychologist in a working-class region is that with those patients who find it difficult using words it is important for therapists to focus on the behavioural modality both within and between sessions. When teaching rational concepts is important with such patients, then it is essential to use the visual mode of communication as an adjunct to the verbal mode. Thus, I use pen and paper a lot, sketching disgrams to facilitate such patients' understanding of difficult rational concepts. In addition, I have devised a number of visual models to illustrate rational concepts (Dryden, 1980b). When patients employ words to protect them from emotional experience, i.e. when they employ intellectualization as a major defensive style, then rational-emotive therapists might more effectively focus on the experiential modality helping such patients to acquaint themselves with that mode of experience from which they have shielded themselves. If therapists spend too much time engaging such patients in traditional rational-emotive socratic dialogue then they may well reinforce their patients' defensive style. Such speculations of course need to be tested.

Beutler (1979) has suggested a system which combines therapeutic modalities and styles in determining whether certain therapies are more effective than others with patients on three major patient dimensions. The first dimension is symptom complexity. If symptoms are circumscribed, Beutler (1979) hypothesizes that a greater behavioural focus would be more effective, whereas if they are more complex, then a greater cognitive focus is needed. The second dimension is defensive style. According to Beutler, if the patient utilises an external defensive style, the therapist needs to emphasise the behavioural modality in therapy whereas cognitive interventions are required with patients utilising an internal defensive style. The third dimension taps the degree to which external events are construed as representing a threat to the person's autonomy-reactance. If the patient is high on the reactance dimension, i.e. if he is pre-disposed to view external events as autonomy-endangering, then the therapist would be more productive if she adopted a less directive, more experiential therapeutic style. If the patient is low on this dimension then greater therapist direction with a more behavioural focus is needed. Beutler (1979) reviewed empirical studies relevant to his hypotheses but found only meagre to moderate support for these hypotheses. However, these hypotheses were not tested directly and Beutler's system remains a promising one in that it provides the rational-emotive therapist with some guidelines as to possible variations in style and modality focus with different patients.

In conclusion, it has been shown how RET practitioners employ rational-emotive theory as a guide in their choice of a wide array of therapeutic interventions. In addition, the argument was advanced that RET practitioners had better take into account patient characteristics in making decisions concerning therapeutic style and modality-focus. However, the central purpose of the eclectic RET practitioner remains the modification of faulty inferences and irrational beliefs.

Chapter Nine

A COMPREHENSIVE APPROACH TO SOCIAL SKILLS TRAINING:
CONTRIBUTIONS FROM RATIONAL-EMOTIVE THERAPY

The Rational-emotive approach to social skills training stresses that for long-term change, therapists had better pay detailed attention to clients' beliefs about themselves, other people, and the world. In RET, the targets for change are not only the inferences that patients make about what happens to them at point (A) (Beck and Emery, 1979), but also the way these events are evaluated at point (B).

Rational-emotive theory states that emotional and behavioural consequences at point (C) are largely determined by these evaluations. Rational-emotive therapists conclude that they do not know their clients' goals in advance but "encourage people to choose the kinds of basic values and goals they want and to select self-training in the kinds of skills that will probably more appropriately and efficiently abet their chosen values" (Ellis, 1977h, p. 34). It follows that what is rational in rational-emotive theory are those processes which aid and abet clients to achieve their own goals and what is irrational are those processes which hinder the achievement of these goals. While it may be true that the skills which social skills trainers help their clients acquire may abet their own personally-held goals, it is important to recognise that the acquisition of these skills in the therapeutic situation are not sufficient for clients to achieve these goals.

It is possible to look at the concept of rationality/irrationality in a different way. Ellis (1962) has stressed that a major feature of rational beliefs are that they reflect personal preferences, wants or desires. Rational beliefs become irrational when the patient converts these preferences, wants or desires into absolutistic

musts, oughts, or shoulds. Rational-emotive theory
further hypothesises that a <u>desiring</u> philosophy is
more adaptive and productive than a <u>demanding</u>
philosophy. While Ellis (1977i) has presented evidence in favour of this theory, it should be pointed
out that it is notoriously difficult to operation-
alise these concepts and at present, stating that a
desiring philosophy is more adaptive and productive
than a demanding philosophy should be regarded as a
hypothesis rather than a fact. In this section a
number of therapeutic issues are addressed.
Emphasis will be placed on (a) those beliefs which
clients in social skills groups may hold which
hinder their long-term change and (b) how to change
such beliefs.

1. SELF-ACCEPTANCE VERSUS SELF-ESTEEM

In a recently up-dated list of common irrational ideas (Ellis, 1977j), one such idea is
presented which is central to a rational-emotive
approach to social skills training: "this is the
idea that you can give yourself a global rating as a
human and that your general worth and self-
acceptance depends on the goodness of your performances and the degree that people approve of you".
This idea is considered irrational since rational-
emotive theorists claim that it is not possible to
give such a complex and constantly changing organism
as a human being a single rating. Thus, self-esteem
(which is a variant of self-rating) is considered a
pernicious rather than a helpful concept in social
skills training. Most therapeutic systems do not
consider self-esteem as potentially harmful but
rather hold that it is crucial to raise a client's
level of self-esteem. This may make it difficult
for clinicians to integrate RET into their standard
social skills training practice. As a result,
clinicians may have to rethink their views on the
self-rating/self-acceptance issue and consider the
implications of adopting a self-esteem as opposed to
a self-acceptance philosophy.

But what is meant in practical terms by the
statement that helping a client to improve his self-
esteem may be pernicious? To illustrate this,
consider John, a patient in a social skills training
group. John is assiduous in attenting training
sessions and shows increasing competence at
practicing social skills in the therapeutic
setting. He is encouraged to go out to practice such
skills in his own life setting. He does this by

going to a club and engaging a female in conversation for ten minutes. She responds well to him
and he comes back to the next group session in a
positive frame of mind which the therapist and his
fellow group members reinforce. On the next
occasion, John approaches a woman in an optimistic
frame of mind. He begins to engage her in conversation but after two minutes the woman, who has
not responded to him, excuses herself and leaves.
John becomes depressed and in a discouraged mood
misses the next two group meetings. When he finally
returns, exploration of this interaction reveals a
number of interesting phenomena. The therapist
discovers that John had concluded that because the
woman showed no interest to him and excused herself
so soon after he initiated the contact, this was
proof that he was really unlikeable. Indeed,
further exploration revealed that John had
concluded that he was likeable when the first female
responded to him so warmly. John is thus making
global ratings of himself dependent upon the responses he gets from significant others in his environment. In RET, we would uncover and challenge
the notion that, (i) it is valid to make such global
ratings, and (ii) that such self-ratings are dependent upon the responses of significant others.
Rather John had better be taught that he could
accept himself as a fallible human being with poor
(but improving) social skills, whether or not other
people in his social milieu responded well to him.
Ellis (1977h) has argued that he " . . . as an RET
practitioner, invariably not only shows shy, non-
encountering individuals that they don't have to
succeed at social relations or view it as awful or
terrible and themselves as worthless persons if they
fail, but simultaneously gets them to try various
ways of relating so that they will see how they can
bear failure and not put themselves down" (p. 31).
    The above statement reveals that it is
important to fully prepare clients to evaluate themselves rationally when they fail (as they un-
doubtedly will) to either implement their newly
acquired social skills in the outside world, or to
gain positive responses from others. Indeed, using
the technique of reframing (Watzlawick, 1978),
rational-emotive therapists can help clients see
the positive features in such failure experiences,
in that these experiences give them opportunities to
accept themselves in the face of adversity. Helping
clients to adopt a self-acceptance philosophy
rather than a self-esteem philosophy will encourage

them to seek out experiences which they might other-wise avoid. However, it is important to state that the hypothesis that therapeutic procedures based on a self-acceptance philosophy are more successful long-term than therapeutic procedures based on a self-esteem philosphy, needs to be empirically assessed.

2.   COMPETENCE-RELATED BELIEFS

In working with clients in social skills train-ing, trainers are usually struck by their strong tendency to evaluate themselves negatively as a consequence of failing to live up to a certain standard of competence in carrying out homework assignments. In believing that they must be thoroughly competent at putting their newly acquired social skills into practice, these clients become either very depressed as a result of failing or will avoid the practice that is important in helping them to achieve their social goals. A major task of rational-emotive therapists in this aspect of social skills training is to help clients dispute the belief that they must be thoroughly competent. In doing so, therapists had better help clients adhere to the more rational belief "I want to be competent in putting my newly acquired skills into practice, but if I don't it's hardly catastrophic". It is often observed that such clients, as therapists begin to dispute their irrational beliefs, conclude falsely that "It doesn't matter whether I succeed or not". Therapists had better watch this drift from defining something as "all important" to defining it as "unimportant" and had better help clients acknowledge that it does matter whether they achieve their standards and as a result will be disappointed in their failure to do so. Consequently clients will be helped to see that they can be disappointed but not devastated as a result of failing to achieve their own perfectionistic standards. At the same time, it is important for therapists to spend a lot of time helping clients lower their perfectionistic standards and thus help them (i) to view themselves as fallible persons who can set themselves more realistic human goals and (ii) to accept themselves as fallible persons even if they fail to reach these more realistic goals.
Increased social competence is not just a matter of learning and practicing the various component skills which are taught in traditional social skills training. Both the timing of skill

responses and the way skills are smoothly put together are important features which may determine whether significant others will respond favourably or not to the clients in everyday life. In order to improve their skills at correctly timing social responses and thus become smoother in the meshing of these component skills, clients had better throw themselves into social interactions at every opportunity. It is hypothesized that if clients adhere to the rational belief that "It is unfortunate but hardly catastrophic if I do not achieve the level of competence that I would ideally like", then they will be more likely to persevere in the face of adversity than if they adhere to the irrational standpoint that they must achieve their standards. Although clients will be more likely to persevere in practicing new social skills if they are able to accept themselves for slower progress than desired, there is another important reason why they may avoid the hard work of practice.

3.   DISCOMFORT-RELATED BELIEFS

Ellis (1979g) has made an important contribution to rational-emotive theory by distinguishing between two distinct, but often interrelating, forms of anxiety. The first, Ego Anxiety (EA), results when patients demand that they achieve certain standards or gain approval and consequently evaluate themselves negatively for failing to achieve these goals. The two above mentioned processes - i.e. global self-ratings and demands for competence - are characteristic features of ego anxiety and serve to maintain it. A conceptually different form of anxiety - Discomfort Anxiety (DA) results from clients' absolute demand that they achieve a certain level of comfort in their lives. Discomfort Anxiety may be present on its own, as in the case of Ron who had gone a long way to accept himself as a fallible human being but still avoided social encounters because he believed that it was too hard to continue to practice his newly acquired skills in everyday life and that it should be easier to put them into practice. Discomfort anxiety, however, may interact with ego anxiety as with David who evaluated himself negatively as a result of his failure to maintain a conversation with a woman, started to experience anxiety and consequently defined that anxious feeling as too uncomfortable to bear. Thus, discomfort anxiety may serve to interfere with the patient's attempts at disputing his ego anxiety-related beliefs. The task of therapists in this situation is to help such clients deal with their discomfort anxiety-related beliefs before dealing with their ego-anxiety-related beliefs. Rational-emotive therapists aim to show their clients that anxiety is uncomfortable but can be tolerated and often lessened when they adopt an accepting attitude to the experience of that anxiety.

An example will clarify how therapists can help clients who experience both ego and discomfort anxieties. Robert, a university student, was seen in a university health setting, experienced great social anxiety is conversing with both men and women. He also had poor social skills in a number of areas. The therapist proceeded to concurrently help Robert improve his social skills and dispute the belief that he must appear witty and bright and if he didn't then he was an idiot. Robert would characteristically enter social situations and begin to put into practice his newly acquired social skills. However, he would soon excuse himself from such situations when he started to become anxious due to his belief that other people would regard him as a moron because he was not making noteworthy conversation and this indeed would prove that he really was a moron. Robert was helped to dispute such beliefs both in the session, by means of cognitive disputing and imagery related exercises to the point where he was adept at disputing such beliefs within the therapeutic setting. However, Robert was not able, at this point, to dispute such beliefs in-vivo. Discomfort anxiety prevented Robert from disputing this belief in vivo namely: "that it would be terrible to experience such anxiety in social situations and I couldn't bear to". The therapist helped Robert to re-evaluate such anxiety as uncomfortable and to use this feeling of discomfort as a cue to in-vivo disputing. This enabled him to remain in the social situation and to take the risk of speaking up and saying something mundane while accepting himself for doing so.

It is important to realise here that clients often switch their goals as a consequence of discomfort anxiety. For example, a client with a fear of approaching and interacting with an attractive woman may have as his therapeutic goal to ultimately be able to do so. What may interfere with his progress towards this goal will be a competing goal of feeling comfortable in social situations and thus he may quickly switch from one goal to the other once he begins to experience anxiety. Rational-emotive therapists may employ several anxiety-reducing methods to help such persons cope with their anxiety, but would not make the error of employing techniques (which are palliative in nature) if they would reinforce the idea that: "It would be terrible to experience anxiety". Here, rational-emotive therapists aim to help clients adhere to the more rational belief that: "It is better not to experience anxiety, it is uncomfortable and inconvenient if I do but it is not horrible or dreadful and I can stand it".

Discomfort anxiety also arises when clients hold the belief that: "Things should be easy for me". As mentioned above, acquiring a sense of timing and smoothness in complex social performance so that clients are more socially reinforcing to persons in their environment is often an arduous task and involves putting up with a large measure of failure. Clients often deprive themselves of these opportunities precisely because of their discomfort anxiety. A major task of therapists in this situation is to help clients adhere to the more rational "It would be nice if it was easier to get what I want (i.e. desired social success) but it is not and that's frustrating. It really is hard and it should be this hard". Such clients tend to escalate this rational belief to an irrational belief which serves to keep them from the practice that is crucial to goal attainment. An example of such an irrational belief might be: "Forcing myself into the social world and putting up with failure is too hard for me, it would be dreadful if I experienced this and thus it is easier if I avoid doing this". Apart from helping such clients adhere to the more rational belief, it is often helpful to point out to them that they have got their world upside down! When such patients claim that something is hard and imply that avoidance is easy, they are adopting a short-term time perspective in making such evaluations. Implicit in this viewpoint is that it is in fact harder for them, long-term, if they continue to avoid and in fact it is easier, long-term, if they put up with the hard work of practice. Thus, therapists can help clients see that what is hard is easy and what is easy is hard. Needless to say, this is not an easy task and therapists had better overcome their own discomfort anxiety while persisting to help these patients overcome their discomfort anxiety. Ellis (1957) has observed that helping clients overcome their discomfort anxiety is one of the most difficult tasks in therapy!

Another feature of discomfort anxiety is the demand for a guarantee. Often clients refuse to risk entering a social situation because they do not have the certainty that they will meet with success. Such clients demand a guarantee that things will work out well for them, or that they know in advance what will transpire. A rational-emotive therapists named Lemire has come up with a novel way of helping such clients. When clients reveal that they demand a guarantee, Lemire indicates to them that they are in luck. He just happens to have a guarantee in his drawer; would they like it? Clients usually show obvious interest in this therapeutic manoeuvre and generally accept. Lemire then gives him an RET guarantee form on which is written "I guarantee that you will suffer as long as you demand that you have a guarantee". This point additionally emphasises that clients in their willingness to achieve short-term gain condemn themselves to long-term pain. In addition to helping clients gain a different time perspective on the gain/pain ratio, therapists had better lessen some of their short-term pain to un-comfortable but manageable proportions.

A somewhat different form of discomfort anxiety has been described by Maultsby (1975) who has written about the "neurotic fear of feeling a phony". Maultsby notes that often clients do not persist at practicing skills which would ordinarily help them to achieve their goals because at some point in the skill acquisition process, they claim that 'they don't feel themselves'. Such clients may actually report: 'I feel as if I'm not being me'; 'I feel strange and different and I don't like it'; 'What sort of person am I turning into?', etc. Therapists who do not address such issues in social skills training may not be helping their clients achieve their stated goals. It is often sufficient to provide such clients with examples from their own lives where they have felt awkward, felt unnatural, felt that what they were doing was not really them, but where they persisted and acquired new skills. Helping clients see that this is a temporary phase that, if tolerated as an uncomfortable but bearable experience, enables them to persist until newly acquired skills become more natural.

Discomfort anxiety is often a feature in clients' attitudes towards their progress in social skills training. Often such progress is slower than clients would ideally like and it is important that therapists determine if they are defining such slow progress as "undesirable" or as "awful". In addition, ego anxiety may be implicated here. Clients may evaluate themselves negatively for not progressing as quickly as they "should". The following diagram may illustrate how ego anxiety and discomfort anxiety are interwoven in a client's attitude towards slow progress (see Figure 1). Here both ego anxiety and discomfort anxiety lead to avoidance of social situations and thus the client deprives himself of important opportunities to practice social skills. The task of therapists in helping clients overcome either ego anxiety or discomfort anxiety or indeed both is thus to intervene and help clients (1) re-define slow progress as undesirable but bearable and/or (2) accept themselves for their slow progress.

4. APPROVAL-RELATED BELIEFS

Clients with social difficulties are often overconcerned about gaining approval from other people. This over-concern is reflected at two levels: (1) interpretation/misinterpretation of responses from other people; and (2) evaluation of responses from other people. Clients often misinterpret cues from other people in a number of different ways. One major form of distortion involves the interpretation of a neutral response as negative. Here clients try to engage others in conversation, receive a neutral response and as a result conclude that others do not like them. The second major form of distortion occurs when clients receive positive responses from others but distort the message so that the existence of positive responses is denied or explained away. For example, a typical response from clients who receive positive responses from other people is to attribute the other's respones to motives which correspond to their own self-evaluations. To give a clinical example, Ruth was able to talk to a man at a discotheque, yet reported in the following social skills group session that he only spoke to her because he felt sorry for her and wanted to cheer her up. Two major therapeutic strategies are indicated here: first, therapists can use a number of procedures outlined by Beck and Emery (1979)[1] which aim to teach clients to view their inferences as hypotheses. Clients can, by collecting data from the events that took place and other sources, then test these hypotheses. A second and equally important

Social Skills Training

Figure 1

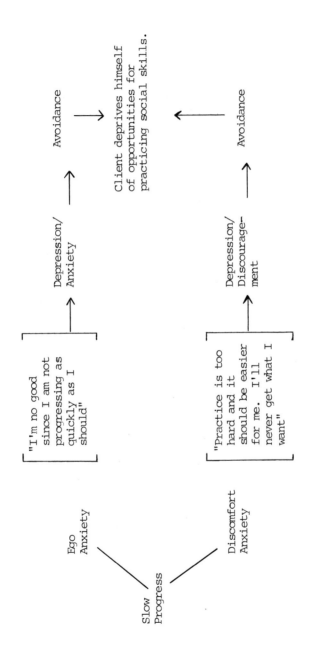

therapeutic strategy involves helping clients identify the self-evaluations implicit in such perceptual distortions and then to dispute these self-evaluations. Thus, Ruth could be shown that she viewed herself as an "unlikeable person" and could then be helped to dispute this notion. She could be encouraged to give up self-rating and to accept herself as a person with likeable and unlikeable aspects.

The forementioned strategies are aimed at helping clients to correct cognitive distortions and are included in a comprehensive approach to RET. Comprehensive RET is sometimes contrasted with classical RET (Walen et al., 1980). In classical RET therapists begin by agreeing with clients' inferences about the event. Thus, responding to Ruth, the therapist might say: "OK, let's assume that you are right and he only wanted to cheer you up". He would then help Ruth identify her emotional experience and hence the beliefs underlying that experience. Thus, in classical RET, therapists aim to identify evaluations and inferences without necessarily challenging the validity of the inference itself. An important research issue emerges here. Does working at the evaluative level, i.e. helping clients to evaluate possible incorrect inferences more rationally lead to clients making more accurate inferences? Little research has been carried out on this issue but such studies are crucial if therapists are to be cost-effective in deciding at which level of cognitive activity to intervene - the inferential or the evaluative. It is probable, however, that helping clients make both more accurate inferences and rational evaluations would be more therapeutically effective than either strategy carried out separately.

Both ego anxiety and discomfort anxiety are often implicated in clients attitudes towards gaining others' approval. Clients often conclude that gaining others' disapproval means that they are worthless or unlikeable, etc. Here, therapists may help the clients see that others' disapproval could occur for a number of reasons which may provide more information about the evaluators than the evaluated. However, even if clients have an unlikeable trait or combination of traits which might be evaluated negatively by most people, is this sufficient proof that such clients are totally worthless or totally unlikeable? Therapists had better recognise that other people may well reject some clients because of their poor social skills, poor

timing of executing such skills and/or an awkwardness of style in social interactions. Thus, it is
probable that clients who persist at practicing
social skills will be rejected as a consequence of
the poor timing and relative awkwardness of their
social performance. It is thus important for
therapists to help these clients accept themselves
with poor social skills, poor timing and awkwardness
of style, if they are to be encouraged to continue
to utilize opportunities to overcome these deficits
and to become more socially adept.

Discomfort anxiety is implicated when clients
indicate that they can't stand the discomfort of
being disliked. Such clients often make continued
attempts to regain the approval of others which
often has the paradoxical result of further alien-
ating others. In RET, clients are shown that while
it is uncomfortable and inconvenient to exist in a
world where people may dislike them, this hardly
constitutes something that they can't stand unless
they foolishly tell themselves that they can't stand
it. Again, it is important to note that clients who
struggle to cope with social rejection and disapproval from others often experience both ego and
discomfort anxieties, which influence each other
often in chain-reaction fashion.

5. ANGER-RELATED BELIEFS

In previous sections we have noted that clients
who endeavour to put into everyday practice the
skills that they have learned in their social skills
groups often experience anxiety and depression as a
result of failing to (a) achieve their own standards
of performance desired and (b) gain desired
responses from other people. However, a smaller
group of clients experience anger at themselves,
other people, and the world as a result of such
failures. The tasks of rational-emotive therapists
are again to (1) identify the demands which are
implicit in such evaluations towards self, others
and the world and (2) help clients replace such
demands with more rational preferences. It is
important to note that rational-emotive therapists
make a crucial theoretical distinction between cognitive determinants of anger and annoyance. Anger
is said to follow from demands not being met, while
annoyance is said to result when desires are
thwarted. Thus rational-emotive therapists would
not necessarily help clients change beliefs which
underpin annoyance since such beliefs are deemed

rational.   Indeed, annoyance is regarded as an
appropriate negative emotion, appropriate in the
sense that it motivates clients to act and change
what they find annoying.

Anger at self occurs when clients fail to
achieve goals which they have defined as essential
to achieve.   It is interesting to note that while
some clients experience depression as a result of
such   failure,   others   experience   anger   at   themselves.   It is thus important for therapists to note
clients' own idiosyncratic emotional 'styles'.

Anger at others often results when clients
demand that since they have learned and are
continuing to practice new social skills then other
people have to respond in a certain way.   Such
clients can be shown that even though they show
diligence at practicing their new skills in everyday
life, there is no law which states that they must
get (i.e. deserve) what they would like - i.e. other
people to respond favourably to them.   It is often
helpful for therapists to explain that as clients
become more socially competent, they will probably
gain more favourable responses from others.   However, even though they may become extremely proficient socially, other people may, and probably
will, reject them despite or even because of this!

Clients   sometimes   experience   anger   towards
their   therapists.   Such   clients   sometimes   put
therapists on a pedestal and believe that therapists
have magic wands which when waved will cure all, or
that   therapists   have   some   magic   called   "Social
Skills Training" which, if put into practice in
everyday life, will bring clients what they want.
Thus, when such clients experience failure they may
put the blame on their therapists since it is their
fault that clients are not getting what they want.
Such   anger   directed   towards   therapists   is   often
defensive in nature in that clients would blame
themselves for failing if they were not to blame
their therapists.   However, such anger may not be
defensive in nature and may be related to clients
beliefs towards authorities who should be able to
deliver what they have promised, or what they are
perceived to have promised.

Lastly, clients may experience general anger
towards the world for treating them unfairly in
bringing them suffering and denying them favourable
responses from others.   A related belief reflects
the   unfairness   concerning   clients'   social
difficulties. Statements like: 'Why me?', or 'Why
should   I   have   to   be   the   one   to   have   social

problems?' are often heard. Such anger directed towards the world is based on the core underlying assumption that the world should be fair. If therapists explore this in more detail they often find that such clients really mean that the world should be fair TO THEM! Clients can be shown that while inherent fairness or justice in the world would be greatly desired, there is plenty of evidence that such justice does not exist and while this may be frustrating it hardly constitutes a horror unless so defined. Quite often it is helpful to point out that while clients focus on certain unfairnesses which are to their disadvantage, they often do not focus on other unfairnesses which are to their advantage. Thus for example, a client with poor social skills who dwells on the unfairness that he is the one who experiences social problems may at the same time be asked to focus on the unfairness that he is more intelligent than most people. It is indeed rare to meet clients in clinical settings who are depressed or angry at the world because they are being treated so (unfairly) well!

In the preceding four sections, it has been shown how clients' inaccurate inferences and irrational evaluations deter them from putting newly acquired social skills into practice in their everyday lives. In doing so it was demonstrated how RET in particular can help therapists' understanding of clients who not only approach social situations with poorly developed skills but also with a whole range of cognitions, some which aid, while others hinder them reaching their social goals. Suggestions were made to aid therapists in their endeavours to help clients change those cognitions which serve as barriers to goal achievement.

NOTE

1. A comprehensive discussion of procedures that are aimed to help clients correct their cognitive distortions is beyond the scope of this chapter. Readers are referred to Beck and Emery (1979).

Chapter Ten

PSYCHOANALYTIC   PSYCHOTHERAPY   FOR   DEPRESSIVE
PATIENTS: CONTRIBUTIONS   FROM   COGNITIVE-RATIONAL
THERAPY

Whiteley (1981) reported on his experiences of
running   group   therapy   sessions   with   depressive
patients along psychoanalytic lines. He concluded
that   since   the   overall   experience   was   an   unproductive   one,   the   treatment   of   depressive
patients   may   still   be   best   carried   out   using
individual therapy. He noted that in the group
therapy sessions his interpretations were seen as
criticisms or confrontations and thus presumably of
little value to the group members.   Moreover he
hypothesized   that   his   depressive   patients'
behaviour in the group was motivated by anxiety
concerning   (1) attack   by   other   group   members;
(2) being   rejected,   and   (3) disapproval.
Therapists of many different persuasions have noted
the same distorted patterns of cognition in depressive patients.   I will argue in this paper that
recent advances in rational-emotive therapy and the
cognitive therapy of depression (Beck et al., 1979)
may provide important guidelines for the practice of
psychoanalytic   psychotherapy   of   depressive
patients.

DEVELOPING THE OBSERVING SELF

Weiner   (1975)   has   made   an   important   distinction   between   the   experiencing   self,   which
processes information and has affective reactions
consequent to this 'cognitive' activity and the observing self - the part of the self which can
reflect on the experiencing self's psychological
processes.   Effective   therapy   involves   helping
patients to shift between these two 'sub-selves' as
the occasion requires.   One of the major problems
highlighted in Whiteley's (1981) report may have
been his inability, given the treatment context, to

help his patients to best utilize their observing selves. It seemed to me that his patients were not sufficiently trained to utilize their observing capacities prior to group therapy or if they were so trained, then the intensity of the treatment context was such as to make utilization extraordinarily difficult.

Beck et al. (1979) have stressed in their book, Cognitive Therapy of Depression, the importance of deliberately and systematically training patients to become expert observers of their cognitive processes since certain cognitive phenomena are deemed to be centrally implicated in their depressive reactions. Initially, cognitive therapists train patients to become aware of their 'stream of consciousness' thoughts, i.e. those that are readily available to identification. These are termed "automatic thoughts" by Beck et al. Cognitive therapists systematically help patients to fully develop their skill at identifying automatic thoughts and encourage them to regard such thoughts as hypotheses about reality rather than accurate statements about reality. Patients are then trained to examine such thoughts and to respond to them if they prove to be based on cognitive distortions. However, automatic thoughts are but the tip of the "cognitive iceberg", and are based on underlying evaluative assumptions which are only formulated later on in therapy as part of a joint enterprise between patient and therapist. The formulation of such underlying assumptions depends on the collection of sufficient numbers of automatic thoughts to make such formulation possible. Cognitive therapists then do not generally make interpretations to patients but help patients to collect and examine data (automatic thoughts) and from there to make their own interpretations of the underlying meaning of such data. Although Whiteley's (1981) interpretations may have been accurate, his patients may not have been sufficiently helped to process either the information contained within them or their cognitive reactions to him as group therapist making interpretations. Deliberate attempts to train depressive patients to become skilled observers and examiners of their cognitive processes is best done initially by employing their own experiences outside therapy as data for examination. Cognitive therapists help patients talk about and reflect on their weekly outside experiences before dealing with any transference data that may emerge. According to this view, therapy with depressed patients based on making transference interpretations without first training patients to observe and examine their cognitions places much faith in their spontaneous ability to utilize their observing selves in the service of therapy. It is apparent that Whiteley's patients' spontaneous ability to utilize their observing selves was limited.

Group cognitive therapy is generally carried out after depressive patients have had some exposure to individual therapy where such deliberate and systematic training has been carried out. If this group treatment mode is used with patients without individual therapy experience, the initial group sessions are devoted to such training again using members' extra-therapy experiences as data. Here group therapists take quite an active stance to ensure that all patients become competent in the observing-examining process.

DEPRESSION AND PSYCHOANALYTIC INTERPRETATIONS

Unfortunately, Whiteley (1981) does not provide examples of the specific interpretations that he made in his therapeutic interventions. Whiteley (personal communication) has said, however:

"I think that the only sorts of interpretations I may have made might have concerned defences such as silence or perhaps depression itself, both of which I saw as a form of safety from interference from outside. I might also have interpreted the lack of involvement amongst members of the group with each other as fear of criticism or attack".

It is apparent from his article that patients did react negatively to his interpretation. In terms of the cognitive model of depression:

Whiteley made an interpretation —— patients made their own negative inferences and evaluations concerning his interpretation and had a concomitant affective response. —— Patients made critical comments about Whiteley's interpretation.

Either no attempt was made to help patients reflect on their inferences and evaluations of Whiteley's remarks or further negative cognitive reactions were forthcoming in response to any such attempts. Thus Whiteley is in a bind. If he makes enquiries about such negative reactions, (a) patients may not have the ability to reflect on the cognitive determinants of their affective reactions, (b) the intensity of the experience may be such as to make such reflection extremely difficult, or (c) Whiteley's interpretation may not account for his patients' depression.

On this last point, since Whiteley was not able to supply me with any specific interpretations he made in his group sessions, I invited a member of the West Midlands Institute of Psychotherapy, a psychoanalytic therapist, to supply me with specific interpretations which had been actually made to depressive patients in the course of their therapy. While I do not wish to generalize from the activity of one psychoanalytic practitioner to others, I do wish to show how such interpretations may not help patients get to the ideological root of their depressive experiences.

Interpretation 1

"I'm inclined to suggest that you've been particularly depressed this week because you've been feeling at odds with various members of your family".

This suggests to the patient that depression is caused by feeling at odds with various family members. Cognitive-rational therapists would disagree and would help the patient distinguish between cognitive evaluations that lead to sadness (e.g. How unfortunate! I wish this was not happening) about the state of affairs and those that lead to depression (e.g. How terrible! I can't stand this conflict!).

Interpretation 2

"I'm thinking now, from what's just been said, that your guilt and depression may be a means by which you try and cope with difficult fantasies about freedom, self-indulgence and escape".

Cognitive-rational therapists would help the patient see the direct relationship between cognitive evaluations about such fantasies and depression/guilt. As an example the patient may first infer that such fantasies are wrong and forbidden and then conclude that he/she was bad for having them. In the actual interpretation made, it is difficult to determine whether the therapist is suggesting that the depression/guilt is a direct response to the fantasies or a way of warding off more dire feelings. If the former, the patient is not helped to see the more direct evaluative link between the fantasies and the feelings of depression and guilt.

123

Interpretation 3
> "It seems from what you just said that you're
> depressed right now because you think you've
> undermined our relationship by criticising me
> last week".

Here the therapist posits that depression stems from
the client's inference that the relationship between them has been undermined following the
criticism. Cognitive-rational therapists would
disagree. They posit that emotions are related to
evaluations not inferences and here the client's
implicit evaluations are missing. It may be that
the client was blaming him/herself for the inferred
event, e.g. "I undermined the relationship. I'm no
good" or "I undermined the relationship, I can't
stand the prospect of being left by my therapist".

In these three examples, the clients are led to
believe that their depression is caused by external
events or their inferences. The cognitive-rational
perspective suggests that this is incorrect, rather
depression is viewed as being determined by cognitive evaluations and that the clients in these
examples are being presented with a jigsaw-puzzle
with the main piece missing.

Interpretation 4
> "It sounds as though you're finding it hard to
> express your anger and disapointment about how
> your therapy is progressing, and its almost as
> if the annnoyance gets turned in on itself".

Here the therapist implies that feelings have
"agency"properties independent of the person: annoyance gets turned in on itself. This may encourage the client's external locus of control at-
tributions which may perpetuate his/her help-
lessness. The cognitive-rational therapist may say
if he used the interpretation format:
> "It sounds as though you're finding it hard to
> express your anger and disappointment about
> how your therapy is progressing. Am I right?
> (If so ——) How do you feel about finding
> expressing such feelings different?

The psychoanalytic therapist's example seems to
suggest that annoyance turned inwards leads to depression. Cognitive-rational therapists would say
that if the client was depressed about not expressing such feelings he may be, for example,
blaming him/herself for such difficulty and/or for
experiencing the feelings in the first place. Here
cognitive evaluations are again stressed in the
depressive emotional episode.

Interpretations 5 and 6

"I don't really think you've resolved your feelings about your mother's loss, and suspect your depression is linked with this somehow".
"You obviously find it hard to express your mixed feelings about your father since his death, despite the fact that the rest of your family practically curse him. It's almost as if you feel only kindness for him and the others feel only anger . . . depression ties up with this".

Here the therapist is making associative links, not causal ones as were made in interpretations 1-3. However, he does not show the clients how depression is linked or tied up with the unresolved feelings in interpretation 5 or the difficulty of expressing mixed feelings in interpretation 6. Cognitive-rational therapists would help the client to specify the cognitive evaluations tht mediate between the conflict and the depression.

The common thread in the above six interpretations is that from a cognitive-rational perspective the therapist has not helped clients to identify the core of their depressing experiences - namely depressive cognitive evaluations. Given different cognitive evaluations the clients could face the same situations or conflicts and experience less troublesome emotions.

CONCLUSION

It seems to me that psychoanalytic psychotherapists can learn two important lessons from cognitive-rational therapists to enhance therapeutic effectiveness with depressive patients. First, they would do well to deliberately train patients to become skilled observers and examiners of their cognitive processes in a more systematic fashion than they are accustomed. Second, they may need to focus more specifically on cognitive evaluations as the ideological root of the depressive experience.

ACKNOWLEDGEMENT

I would like to thank (1) Dr R Whiteley for responding to my enquiries about the experience described in his article, and (2) the West Midlands Institute of Psychotherapy member who provided me with the interpretations discussed in the present article. For reasons of confidentiality, the member will remain anonymous.

Chapter Eleven

RATIONAL-EMOTIVE MARITAL THERAPY: CURRENT PRACTICE
AND WIDENING HORIZONS

Rational-emotive therapy was developed by
Albert Ellis in the mid 1950's in America. While
Ellis as part of his busy private practice sees
clients individually, in groups, and in both marital
and family contexts, the bulk of RET writings has
been devoted to the use of the methods with
individual clients. This is understandable when, as
we shall see later, it is noted that RET theory
tends to emphasise intra-personal determinants of
emotional disturbance and tends to de-emphasise
interpersonal determinants of emotional
disturbance. The purpose of this present paper is
twofold: (a) to outline the theory and practice of
RET as traditionally practised within a marital
context, and (b) to suggest ways in which interpersonal determinants of emotional disturbance can
be given more emphasis in the thinking of RET
therapists as they decide when and how to make
therapeutic interventions.

1.   THE RATIONAL-EMOTIVE VIEW OF MARITAL DYS-
     FUNCTION AND ITS TREATMENT

The rational-emotive view of marital dysfunction holds that such disturbance is determined
chiefly by the unrealistic expectations or beliefs
held by one or both partners. Such beliefs and
expectations are claimed to lead to emotional disturbance and unproductive behaviour. Therapeutic
strategy then for the rational-emotive therapist is
to help one or both partners to change these beliefs
and expectations in the direction of greater
realism. Such beliefs are termed irrational by
Ellis (1962) in the sense that they hinder the
person from obtaining his or her goals. Disturbed
emoting and unproductive behaviour which are seen as

stemming from such irrational beliefs are primarily responsible for goals not being obtained. Thus, the rational-emotive therapist would aim to help both partners to identify long-term goals and then help them to see, (i) how their goals are being sabotaged by holding such irrational beliefs, (ii) the content of such irrational beliefs, and (iii) how these irrational beliefs can be changed so that both partners achieve their goals.

The rational-emotive therapist is guided by the system's theoretical standpoint that such irrational beliefs are characterised by the concept of demandingness which takes three major forms (Lembo, 1976). Thus one partner can hold the following irrational beliefs: (a) demanding that he/she must act or not act in a certain way, (b) demanding that the other partner or other people must not act in a certain way, and (c) demanding that life circumstances or the world must be or not be the way he/she decrees it to be. The rational-emotive therapist in clinical practice seeks to zero in on these demands (which are absolutistic statements in that they allow no margin for error) and endeavours to help the disturbed partner(s) stick with the rational alternative of these beliefs. Rational beliefs involve wishes, wants, desires or preferences which reflect the partner's value system but which do allow for a world in which such wishes are not met. Rational-emotive theory states that if married partners were to stick with their rational beliefs, they would experience negative emotions such as sadness, disappointment, annoyance, regret, frustration, but would not get such debilitating negative emotions such as depression, anxiety, anger or resentment which characterise marital dysfunction. If both partners were operating from a rational belief system they would be more likely to coolly determine whether the differences between them were irreconcilable and thus make a decision to separate or whether such differences were reconcilable in which case they would strive to reconcile them.

Another way of looking at unrealistic or irrational beliefs within a marital context is to consider Sager's (1976) concept of 'contracts'. Sager (1976) has pointed out that spouses often have a series of contracts which can operate on various different levels of awareness. Thus a contract may be acknowledged and expressed, acknowledged but not expressed, and not acknowledged and therefore not able to be expressed. Often the most powerful contracts are those which are neither acknowledged nor expressed. Wessler (1979) has termed such contracts 'Personal Rules for Living' which are similar in nature to Kovacs and Beck's (1978) concept of 'Underlying Cognitive Structures'. What RET has to add to the notion of contracts is that the destructive power of holding such contracts is not just the content of the contract but that the other person must fulfill his or her part of the contract. As will be argued below, somewhat against RET practice and in particular Ellis' promptings, value for both partners may be gained by understanding the past determinants of presently held contracts.

While there is some evidence that marital conflict is related to partners' endorsement of irrational beliefs (Eisenberg and Zingle, 1975, and Epstein et al., 1979), further research is needed to more clearly specify the probable complexity of such a relationship. The two studies that have been carried out in this area have employed paper and pencil tests of belief systems. The use of such tests can be criticised in that the endorsement of irrational or rational belief items on such tests may poorly predict a person's response in more concrete and possibly stressful situations. It behoves researchers in this area to devise more valid ways of assessing spouses' adherence to both rational and irrational belief systems.

2. RATIONAL-EMOTIVE MARITAL THERAPY: PRACTICAL CONSIDERATIONS

Unlike a number of other systems of marital therapy, the traditional rational-emotive approach to marital dysfunction is that the individual and not the relationship is the target of change. Walen et al. (1980) make this clear when they write:
"This viewpoint . . . (that is the individual is a target of change) . . . had better be made clear to the client; they may then understand that you are serving them as two independent adults, and that the goals of counseling are to help each one maximise his happiness, whether this means living with or separating from their partner. Unless you make these goals clear, allegiancies can be blurred and trouble can emerge".
It is then important to assess the agendas and goals of each partner and some of this process is best done with the spouses individually. Conjoint marital sessions are indicated when both partners

have the same agendas, but when serious conflicts of agenda arise it is best to see each partner individually. In practice, however, marital therapists are often faced with a situation where one or both partners in the marriage have unstable goals and ambivalent agendas. As a result it may not be as easy in practice as Walen et al. (1980) assume it is in theory to quickly assess agendas which reflect long-term goals. There is little in the RET literature to help the therapist on this issue.

Ellis (personal communication) has indicated that one of the criteria he employs whether to work with a couple conjointly or the partners individually is whether the partners are comfortable in seeing him as a couple. Thus, if the partners are comfortable in seeing Ellis together he will thus do so. However if they are not comfortable in seeing him together he will then proceed to see them individually.

The advantages of working conjointly in rational-emotive marital therapy are mainly three-fold. First, the therapist can determine from in-session interaction the presence or absence of disturbance in a more valid way than he may be able to if he worked with both partners individually. Thus as systems-oriented therapists maintain, the process is often more revealing than the content of people's reports. Secondly, working conjointly promotes empathic understanding of partners towards one another in a way which may be less likely if partners are not being seen together. The hidden danger here of course is that once one partner learns that the other is largely responsible for creating their own feelings then the former may tend to conclude that after all the mate is the sick one. It is thus important, as will be determined below, for the therapist to show both partners, while working conjointly, that they are responsible for creating their own feelings and not just focus more exclusively on one partner to the exclusion of another. Thirdly, the therapist can model how to identify and dispute irrational beliefs in a non-threatening way so that one spouse can help the other spouse to do this in their every day situation.

3. CONJOINT RATIONAL-EMOTIVE MARITAL THERAPY: MAINTAINING THE WORKING ALLIANCE

Conjoint rational-emotive marital therapy is most frequently conducted with one therapist. The resulting 'holy trinity' leads to problems in maintaining the working alliance. Walen et al. (1980) emphasise this when they say:

"The therapist had better realise that triads are extremely unstable groups which easily break into a dyad and an isolate. Unless the therapist is skillful to avoid it, couples counseling can be perceived by one (or both) partner(s) as the therapist and the mate siding together against a focal client . . . some clients welcome an alliance with the therapist because it 'shows that the client is right'".

Walen et al. go on to say:

"A simple solution to help avoid this trap is to address equal numbers of remarks to each person; show that each is creating their own feelings and that <u>both</u> think irrationally when they blame the other and that blaming leads to anger".

While this is indeed an important objective, there remains no research which demonstrates the rational-emotive marital therapist's ability to achieve such equality. Indeed it might be interesting to speculate that such a situation might be the exception rather than the rule. It could be anticipated that the therapist might spend more time on one partner for a variety of different reasons. First, the therapist may spend more time with the 'identified' client in the dyad and thus perhaps collude with the 'non-identified' client's construction of the problem. In RET it is very easy to do this when one is faced with a host of dysfunctional emotions and behaviours in the one partner and very little disturbance (on the surface) in the other partner. As will be shown below, a systems theory perspective is helpful here in enabling the rational-emotive therapist to avoid falling into any potential traps in dealing with such a situation. Secondly, the rational-emotive marital therapist may focus more attention on one partner because of a perceived similarity with that partner. Thirdly, more time might be spent with a partner of the opposite sex or the same sex dependent upon the therapist's own dynamics. Finally and related to the above, a host of what analytic therapists call 'counter-transference' reasons may operate which lead the rational-emotive marital therapist to unbalance the triad. It is encumbent on rational-emotive marital therapists who are working in a conjoint fashion to closely monitor the way they spend their time and to ascertain possible reasons if such unbalancing occurs.

Given that the therapist is successful in spending roughly half his time working with each partner, the traditional tactic is then to undertake an $ABCD^1$ analysis for each partner. Thus in working with one partner the therapist will endeavour to: (i) identify at point 'A' events (most often a behaviour on the part of the other partner) which acts as a stimulus to the partner's emotional disturbance, (ii) determine the emotional experience which accompanies such an event, (iii) identify the beliefs which determine the emotional experience, and (iv) begin to dispute such beliefs if they turn out to be irrational or unrealistic. Having done this the therapist then turns to the other partner and undertakes an ABCD analysis on his emotional or behavioural problem.

4. PERCEPTUAL DISTORTIONS

Beliefs are evaluative in nature. However unrealistic beliefs are not the only determinant of emotional disturbance. Such disturbance may be brought about by one or both partners' distortions in perceiving events. A common tactic in RET is the process of undertaking an ABCD analysis of the client's problem is to go along with the client's perception of 'A'. 'A' is not only the actual event which occurs but of course the person's construction of the event or inference about what has happened. Such inferences of course may be incorrect. Aaron Beck and his associates (e.g., Beck et al., 1979) have outlined a number of ways of challenging clients' perceptual distortions. Such procedures involve helping clients to more accurately describe events and to detect overgeneralisations, arbitrary inferences, and rigid categorisations which may not tally with what has occurred. In classical RET (Walen et al., 1980) the RET therapist will begin by assuming that 'A' is true and then to dispute such irrational beliefs which are held about that perception of 'A'. In comprehensive RET (e.g., Walen et al., 1980) therapists may employ similar therapeutic strategies as outlined above by Beck et al., normally following the traditional RET approach of assuming 'A' is true. One of the implicit assumptions in a traditional RET approach is that when one is successful at working at the 'B' level, i.e. when clients are successfully helped to dispute their irrational beliefs, they are more likely to perceive reality more accurately. However this implicit assumption has never been tested empirically and must remain a working hypothesis. Rational-emotive therapists would argue that if one begins on working at the validity of a client's perceptions and inferences at 'A', although the therapist may be successful at helping the person perceive reality more accurately and thus become less disturbed emotionally and act more function-ally, the client is not helped to dispute irrational beliefs which may be latent and which may emerge should the client's original perception of 'A' become accurate. It may also be possible (even though rational-emotive therapists would doubt this) that helping clients to perceive 'A' more accurately leads in itself to change in beliefs. Again this is an empirical question.

A strategy which is not generally employed in rational-emotive marital therapy but is one which is used more frequently by 'object-relations' therapists is the correction of perceptual dis-tortions by linking current perceptions to their childhood determinants. Thus for example, a wife may conclude that her husband may be acting ag-gressively from insufficient evidence and may be helped to see that her tendency to see men as being aggressive when they are in fact being assertive stems from her early interactions with significant male others. Ellis tends to be rather forceful in his view that exploration of a client's past be generally avoided or dealt with minimally. However other rational-emotive therapists (e.g. Dryden, 1979) suggest that such exploration of past interactions may have therapeutic value in cor-recting present perceptual distortions. Again this can be tested empirically.

Further therapeutic value lies in exploring the past determinants of a spouse's present per-ceptions in the presence of the other partner. It may promote empathic understanding in the one partner towards the other. Thus if the husband in the above example can perhaps understand that his wife's reaction to his assertiveness is based on her early interactions with male significant others, then he may in fact respond differently when she does react negatively to what he deems to be his reasonable behaviour.

5.   SYSTEMS THEORY AND BEHAVIOURAL INTERVENTIONS

Rational-emotive therapists have for a long time recognised the importance of the role of action in the change process. Just helping clients dispute irrational beliefs in the session, cognitively, will be far less efficient than such a process allied with the client going out and acting differently in the world. Thus RET therapists may utilise most of the procedures currently adopted by behavioural marital therapists, such as contingency contracting, communication training, negotiation skill training, etc. While such procedures do seem to have therapeutic potency (Weiss, 1978), RET therapists are sceptical of helping couples learn such skills without helping them to make appropriate changes in their belief systems. The danger for the rational-emotive marital therapist is that such behavioural interventions lead to changes in 'A' and that as each partner's behaviour changes, opportunities to help respective spouses make appropriate cognitive changes in response to their partner's prior obnoxious behaviour are missed. Rational-emotive marital therapists are more likely to institute such procedures after some degree of cognitive disputation has taken place (Ellis, 1977h). Again several empirical questions arise from this controversy. Firstly, to what extent do such behavioural interventions such as communication training, negotiation skills training, etc. bring about lasting cognitive changes? Secondly, what is the therapeutic potency of cognitive disputing in the total process of a cognitive-behavioural approach to marital therapy? Emmelkamp et al. (1978) have in an unrelated field (the treatment of agoraphobics) casted doubt on the therapeutic potency of cognitive disputing without behavioural interventions. However the unanswered question is what does cognitive disputing add to behavioural interventions in the resolution of marital conflict? These questions need to be answered empirically from both short-term and long-term change perspectives.

Because of its emphasis on the intra-personal determinants of emotional disturbance, RET has tended to downplay the impact of interpersonal factors on the development and maintenance of emotional disturbance and dysfunctional marital interaction. Rational-emotive marital therapists are distrustful of behavioural interventions as noted above because they fear that such interventions might bring about quick changes in 'A' which may preclude working at promoting changes of belief. They are similarly sceptical of changes brought about by systems-theory inspired marital approaches (e.g. Sluski, 1978) for the same reasons. This unfortunately has led RET therapists to neglect some of the more helpful insights which a systems perspective can offer, particularly from the point of view of the choice and timing of interventions. One major problem in undertaking an ABCD analysis (as described above) in working with partners separately within a conjoint framework is that the therapist may successfully dispute a belief and promote behaviour change in one partner which has a significantly negative impact on the other partner. The problem here is intervening prematurely, before one has gained an understanding of complex behaviour sequences and their reciprocal influences. Consider the following marital interaction sequence as outlined by Feldman (1976) (See figure 1). Let us assume that the rational-emotive marital therapist is seeing this couple conjointly and begins the session by working with the depressed wife and elicits sequence A(i), B(i) and C(i), where in response to her husband's undermining behaviour the wife puts herself down, and becomes depressed. Let us further assume the therapist is successful in helping the wife to not put herself down in response to her husband's undermining behaviour and proceeds to encourage her to assert herself. At one level the husband concurs that he would in fact welcome such self-assertive behaviour from his wife and she is thus encouraged as a homework assignment to do this before the next session. The couple return the following week even more discouraged because as can be predicted in A(iv), B(iv), C(iv), the wife's self-assertive behaviour has in fact led to the husband putting himself down which leads to further undermining behaviour on his part. Consequently the wife feels trapped and becomes depressed once again. The point here is not that a systems approach to marital therapy and rational-emotive marital therapy are incompatible but that a systems approach can present a wider perspective for rational-emotive marital therapists to enable them to avoid intervening precipitously or inappropriately in a way which brings about unforseen and unwanted consequences. Thus it is perhaps important that

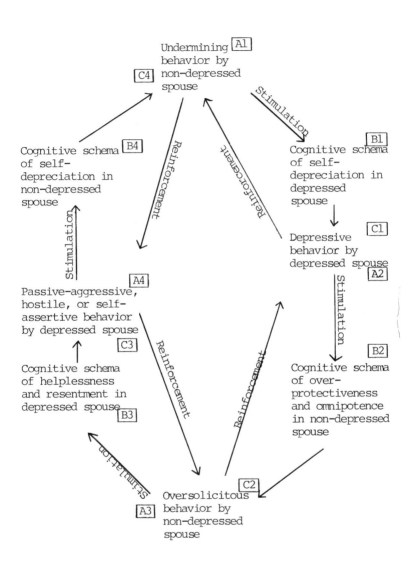

rational-emotive marital therapists broaden their own perspective and consider marital interaction from a wider systems perspective which will help them plan their therapeutic interventions with foresight.

CONCLUSION

In this paper, the rational-emotive approach to marital therapy as traditionally practiced has been outlined together with it's theoretical under-pinnings. Ways in which the practice of rational-emotive marital therapy might be enhanced were put forward drawing from some of the work advocated by object relations, behavioural and more particularly systems theory practitioners in the field of marital therapy. It was argued that the incorporation of such procedures would enrich the practice of rational-emotive marital therapy without it losing its unique focus of aiding spouses in dysfunctional marriages to change their individually held beliefs.

NOTE

A = an event or the perception of an event.
B = Belief.
C = Emotional or behavioural consequence (of B).
D = Disputing irrational beliefs.

Chapter Twelve

AUDIOTAPE SUPERVISION BY MAIL: A RATIONAL-EMOTIVE
PERSPECTIVE

The aims of this chapter are: (1) to describe
my approach to supervising by mail the audiotaped
therapy   sessions   of   novice   rational-emotive
therapists and (2) to discuss some of the issues
that arise from this mode of supervision.
The rational-emotive theory of emotions posits
that emotional experience is based on evaluative
thinking.   Two major types of such thinking are
identified: rational   and   irrational.   Rational
evaluations refer to appraisals of liking or dis-
liking which are stated as personal preferences.
Irrational evaluations occur when these personal
preferences are escalated to unqualified, absolute
demands.   Such demands can be made on ourselves,
other people and the world.   When people rationally
desire or prefer something, they further conclude
that if they don't get it: (a) it is really inconvenient but not the end of the world and (b) they
are fallible humans with failings and inadequacies,
but   not   worthless,   damnable   individuals.
Consequent to holding this rational belief they will
feel frustrated, concerned, sad or sorry -emotions
which are self-enhancing since they are likely to
motivate the individuals to try and change the
situation or help them to adjust if change is not
possible.   However, when people escalate their
preferences to demands, namely that since they want
something, they absolutely must get it, they will
further conclude: (a) it is awful if they don't get
it and (b) they are worthless or bad people for
failing.   Consequent to holding this irrational
belief, they are likely to experience anxiety, depression, shame and guilt - emotions which are self-
defeating in that they generally impede people from
changing the situation and adapting, if change again
is not possible.   Rational-emotive theory further

posits that individuals can take an almost limitless range of desires, e.g. for love, approval, comfort, control, competence and clarity and escalate these to absolute demands. Furthermore, dysfunctional behavioural patterns are deemed to stem from those irrational beliefs.

As I have mentioned elsewhere, the major tasks of the rational-emotive therapist are: "(1) to help the patient to share his theoretical stance that the patient's disturbance has attitudinal antecedents, (2) to help the patient see that changes in belief will promote emotional and behavioural well-being and (3) to help the patient acknowledge that he had better continually work at changing his irrational beliefs by cognitive, imaginal and behavioural disputations." (Dryden, 1982c, p. 17).

The major tasks of rational-emotive supervisors, whether they are supervising novice therapists in person or by mail are: (1) to give them feedback on their understanding of the fundamentals of rational-emotive theory as this is manifested in clinical interventions and (2) to give them feedback on more general clinical skills (Wessler and Ellis, 1980). This dual purpose is implicit in the work of rational-emotive supervisors no matter what training programme novice therapists are undertaking.

Most of my supervision work of novice rational-emotive therapists occurs with those who are undergoing the associate fellowship training scheme which is sponsored by the Institute of Rational-Emotive Therapy in New York. In order to qualify for this programme, novice therapists must: (a) have participated in a five-day primary certificate programme in the fundamentals of rational-emotive therapy and (b) hold a recognised counselling, psychology or psychotherapy qualification in the country in which they are employed. To gain associate fellow status, candidates have to (a) participate in two five-day workshops where various topics in advanced rational-emotive theory and practice are covered and (b) submit twenty-five of their therapy tapes for supervision. Furthermore their supervisors must testify as to their competence. Candidates are strongly encouraged to submit their tapes to no less than three supervisors, although this regulation may be waived in countries which do not have many accredited supervisors, like England. My experience in supervising novice therapists has been almost exclusively limited to supervision of tapes by mail. I have supervised therapists from London, Dublin, Bristol, Nova Scotia in Canada and various cities in America. The working alliance between myself and novice therapists in these programmes is founded on the assumption that I will be giving them feedback on their tapes from a rational-emotive perspective. I encourage supervisees to send me, according to their opinion, both good and bad examples of their work. Occasionally, supervisees only select tapes from therapies that are going well. In this event, I usually confront such supervisees asking them to reflect on the possible underlying motivations for such behaviour, e.g. need for approval, need to be seen as competent, etc.

Whether I am supervising trainees in person or by mail, I believe that listening to audiotapes of therapy sessions is paramount to the process of supervision, especially in rational-emotive therapy. Listening to tapes allows me to hear what therapists say, how they say it, when they say it, and if they say it (Garcia, 1976). In my experience, novice therapists' accounts of therapy sessions are also important for supervisors to elicit, but on their own do not provide adequate information concerning what actually transpired in the sessions. Obviously videotapes of therapy sessions would provide the non-verbal channel missing from audiotapes. However, such technology is expensive and tape compatibility problems that exist mean that videotape supervision by mail is not feasible.

The obvious disadvantage of supervising audio-taped therapy sessions by mail is that the immediate dialogue that face-to-face supervision provides is missing. I find that while I endeavour to ask supervisees questions while taping my supervisory comments, I experience a tendency to give my own opinions about the therapy session more frequently than I would in face-to-face supervision. On this point, I agree with Garcia (1976) who has said: "It seems to me that you are a good supervisor not by the answers you give but by the questions you ask".

Another major disadvantage of supervision by mail is that there is an inevitable delay between trainees conducting therapy sessions and receiving supervision on them. I endeavour to supervise tapes on the day I receive them or no later than the day after receipt. However, it is still doubtful that supervisees will receive my supervision before seeing their clients again.

On the other hand, there are advantages to supervising audiotapes by mail. First, it enables trainees to receive comments on their work where distance precludes face-to-face supervision. It is unrealistic to expect one of my supervisees from Dublin, for example, to fly over for a one-hour supervision session, there being no rational-emotive supervisors in Dublin. Second, it enables trainees to get feedback from a supervisor with a good reputation where distance is again a problem. Thus, if I was limited to face-to-face supervision I would not have been supervised by Albert Ellis as part of my own training programme. Third, this form of supervision allows supervisors to conduct supervision at times convenient to them. Thus, I prefer to supervise tapes late at night at a time when I feel most creative.

There are three major ways of supervising audiotapes by mail. Supervisors can (1) listen to an entire session and then either write or tape their comments; (2) give ongoing written or taped comments while listening to the session, and (3) listen to the entire session first, give general comments and then listen to the session again giving ongoing supervision. My own preference is to tape my comments and provide whatever type of supervision my supervisees find most helpful and can financially afford.

Since I am supervising tapes by mail, I find it even more important to involve my trainees in the supervisory process as much as I can. More specifically I encourage them to formulate their own goals for supervision. I thus ask them at the beginning of our supervisory relationship what they would like to achieve from my supervision and more specifically I encourage them to address themselves to concrete concerns about a particular therapy session. I ask them to specify what strengths they demonstrated in the therapy session and how, in retrospect, they would have conducted the session differently. I prefer my supervisees to send me several tapes from a particular ongoing therapy case rather than to send me isolated tapes from several cases. This helps me to hear how my trainees conduct therapy over time and allows me to address this issue in my supervisory feedback. My overall strategy, then, is to stimulate my supervisees' thinking so that they can learn in time to supervise themselves. However, I do believe that it is important for even experienced therapists to remain in supervision throughout their career. Thus, I have a co-supervisory relationship with a colleague in Chicago with whom I regularly exchange tapes for supervision.

THERAPEUTIC ALLIANCE: A FRAMEWORK FOR SUPERVISION

The framework I use for supervising novice rational-emotive therapists is one based on recent theorizing on the three dimensions of the therapeutic alliance (Dryden, 1982c). From this viewpoint, effective therapy of whatever orientation occurs when: (1) the therapist and client have a good working interpersonal relationship: (the BOND dimension); (2) both therapist and client are working together towards helping the client realise his/her goals: (the GOAL dimension) and (3) both therapist and client acknowledge their respective tasks and believe that such tasks are sufficient for the client to reach such goals: (the TASK dimension).

1. Feedback on therapeutic 'bonds'

In giving my supervisees feedback on the quality of the therapeutic bond between them and their clients, I initially address myself to the core therapeutic conditions described by Rogers (1957). First, I pay attention to therapist empathy. I listen in particular to: (a) whether my supervisees encourage their clients to fully state their problems as they see them; (b) whether and how accurately they communicate such understanding - i.e. do they work from their clients' data or do they allow rational-emotive theory to inappropriately distort such data. Second, I listen closely to the extent to which they accept their clients as fallible human beings - are there any signs that they adopt a judgmental attitude toward their clients? Third, I listen for signs that they are not being genuine in their encounters with their clients - are they inappropriately adopting a facade?

It is important to realise that Rogers' (1957) original hypothesis stated that the important mechanism for change was the extent to which such therapist-offered conditions are perceived by clients rather than by external observers (in this case, supervisors). Nevertheless, if supervisors put themselves in a particular client's frame of reference, such feedback may have increased reliability. I not only give my supervisees feedback on these attitudes but also ask them to reflect on what intrapsychic obstacles might exist

141

in them that could block the therapeutic expression of such attitude. Here, as elsewhere on similar matters, the supervisees are left to do such reflection on their own (or perhaps with their own therapists!)

I then address myself to the extent to which supervisees have developed a collaborative working relationship with their clients. Here I use the concept of 'collaborative empiricism' developed by Beck et al.'s (1979) work in cognitive therapy. The therapeutic style of collaborative empiricism is one in which therapists endeavour to explain to clients the rationale for most of their interventions. Therapists and clients set an agenda at most sessions. Therapists help their clients identify and question maladaptive cognitions through guided discovery. They frequently pause and ask for feedback from clients to determine the impact of their therapeutic interventions, and basically clue clients into most of what is happening in the therapeutic endeavour. I particularly listen for instances where my supervisees do not involve their clients in this way and ask them to reflect on whether this indicates a lack of skill in this area or the presence of dysfunctional attitudes such as low frustration tolerance.

I next concern myself with the question of whether my supervisees' interactive styles present clients with opportunities to reflect on their own dysfunctional interpersonal styles or whether in fact the interactive styles of supervisees actually reinforce their clients' interpersonal problems. For example, while rational-emotive therapy is an active-directive form of psychotherapy, it is possible for the therapist to become too active which is contra-indicated particularly with a passive client since it tends to reinforce the client's passivity and hence his/her personal and interpersonal problems.

Lastly, I listen for signs of anxiety in my supervisees' interaction with clients and try to help them identify its' attitudinal determinants. In my experience, common therapist problems in this area revolve around the following issues: therapist need for client approval, therapist need for competence and to be right, and therapist need to control the interaction. The effects of such irrational beliefs are invariably harmful for clients and early termination, client deterioration and interminable therapy are the common manifestations of these therapist problems. In such cases, I usually recommend that the supervisee in question seeks psychotherapeutic help to resolve such obstacles to the conduct of effective therapy.

2. Feedback on 'goals'

Effective therapy is deemed to occur when therapist and client work toward realizing the client's goals. Thus, first, I listen to hear whether my supervisees have elicited their clients' goals for change. Since this often involves considerable negotiation between therapist and client, I listen for signs that supervisees initiate such negotiation and focus on how they handle the process which usually occurs at the initial stage of therapy. I also listen to hear whether supervisees help their clients to set goals for a particular session and whether attainment of such goals are feasible. In my experience, effective rational-emotive therapists help their clients see that they can reach their ultimate goals by means of reaching a series of mediating goals. I thus listen for client goals at three levels: (1) session goals, (2) mediating goals, and (3) ultimate goals, and most importantly I listen for evidence that therapists help their clients see the links between them.

The major danger of setting goals at the initial stage of rational-emotive therapy is that therapists then assume that these goals are relevant to clients for the entire course of therapy. Since their relevance often becomes outdated, I listen for evidence that supervisees periodically review client goals, and whether they strive to understand the psychological processes underlying the shifts that occur.

I listen to what level of goal specificity supervisees are prepared to work with. Clients can state their goals very broadly e.g. 'I want to be happy' or very specifically e.g. 'I want to meet three girls by August 24th'. Therapist errors occur at both levels of specificity. I encourage novice therapists to consider the value of medium range goals e.g. "I want to be able to approach girls, still feel concerned about being rejected but without feeling devastated by the prospect".

Lastly I listen for evidence that therapists have accepted goals that realistically cannot be achieved by therapy. In my experience as a supervisor these form two clusters. The first cluster of unrealistic goals accepted by therapists are those that would be more appropriate for computers not humans. Thus, clients, whose goals are never to feel anxiety, depression, anger, or who always want to be happy are doomed to disappointment by even the most talented therapist. The second cluster of unrealistic client goals accepted by therapists involve changes in other people or circumstances. This area is more complicated because therapists had better help clients try to non-manipulatively influence others and circumstances where appropriate without appearing to promise that such changes are possible. Thus, I encourage my supervisees to help clients deal with unchanging others or circumstances first before discussing attempts to bring about change in them. This point is particularly pertinent to the field of marital therapy.

3. <u>Feedback on 'tasks'</u>

The tasks of rational-emotive therapists can be grouped into a number of major clusters. The first important cluster of tasks are concerned with <u>structuring</u> therapy. When listening to tapes, I focus and comment on how supervisees structure therapy for their clients. Most specifically, I listen to whether and how supervisees execute the following tasks: (1) the task of outlining their own tasks and that of their clients in therapy; (2) the task of specifying the boundaries that exist that frame therapeutic work (e.g. time, geography, frequency of contact and finance; and (3) the task of eliciting and dealing with clients' expectations and misconceptions about therapy. I further concern myself with how supervisees structure each particular therapy session. Questions that are at the forefront of my mind here are: (a) do therapists set an agenda and/or help clients prioritize items and how do they do this?; (b) do they use the agenda in a flexible way, dealing with important items that emerge during the course of the session or do they stick rigidly to the agenda, no matter what?; (c) do they deal with their clients' experiences concerning any homework assignments arising from the prior session and in particular elicit and deal with reasons for non-completion of such assignments?; (d) do they elicit their clients' cooperation throughout the session and elicit feedback from clients during and at the end of the session?; and (e) do they explain their rationale for the interventions that they have made in the session or do they intervene without ex-planation?

The second cluster of tasks concerns assess-ment. Effective rational-emotive therapy depends heavily on adequate assessment of client problems. Thus, I pay a lot of attention to this phase of therapy. Assessment is best carried out in RET when therapists ask clients for specific examples of their problems. Having elicited specific examples of their clients' problems, including the most relevant inferences about the pertinent activating events, therapists preferably should turn their attention to elicit clear statements of clients' emotional experiences. Vague formulations of emotional experiences, such as "I felt upset" or "I felt bad" are to be avoided, since they do not provide enough clarity for identification of mediating irrational beliefs. If clients' problems are behavioural in nature, clear assessment of behavioural patterns is indicated. Therapists preferably should then proceed to help their clients see that irrational beliefs underlie their dys-functional emotional experiences and/or behavioural patterns. I then listen for evidence that therapists elicit their clients reactions to this formulation of their problems. I give clear feedback to supervisees concerning their errors at this stage, since mistakes here are bound to lead to road-blocks later on in the session. Since a limited number of irrational beliefs are likely to underlie many client problems, I listen for evidence that therapists help their clients see links between their problems, thus enabling clients to begin to assess their own problems in rational-emotive terms.

Another important component in this cluster concerns assessment of client progress on all pertinent problems. Ongoing assessment of progress can be included as an ever-present item on the therapeutic agenda or periodic review sessions can be conducted. Novice rational-emotive therapists often do not carry out this ongoing assesment and thus lose track of their clients' current status. I thus often recommend that my supervisees do this routinely. Ongoing assessment has the additional advantage of providing opportunities for re-formulation of client goals. One particular feature of assessment that novice therapists often overlook is thorough assessment of suicidal ideation and intent in depressed patients. If it is dealt with at all, therapists are often wary of dealing with this issue directly, preferring to ask such questions as: "Have you thought of doing something

silly?" Listening to how therapists deal with
suicide issues often reveals their own distorted
inferences and irrational beliefs concerning these
issues. I thus frequently ask my supervisees to
reflect on their own possible dysfunctional
attitudes concerning introducing the topic of
assessing suicidal ideation and intent. They report
such attitudes as: "I didn't want to upset the
client", "I was too embarrassed to talk about it"
and "I didn't want to put ideas into her head".
When such attitudes are expressed, an ongoing period
of dialogue is highly desirable and if feasible I
encourage the supervisee in question to telephone me
so this can occur. If this is not feasible then I
recommend that my supervisee contacts a clinician
who is experienced in treating suicidal clients for
consultation.

     The third cluster of tasks concerns helping
clients to re-examine distorted inferences and
irrational beliefs. Ideally, therapists involve
clients in this process as much as possible by means
of socratic dialogues. The purpose here is to
stimulate clients' own thinking concerning the dysfunctional nature of their cognitive processes.
Common novice errors here usually involve
therapists explaining to their clients why an
inference is distorted or why a belief is irrational
and providing them with plausible alternatives
instead of allowing those clients who are capable of
performing this task to re-examine for themselves
the untenable bases for these dysfunctional cognitions. Particularly while therapists engage
their clients in the process of re-examining their
irrational beliefs, I listen for evidence that they
help their clients see the link between the
alternative rational belief and their realistic
goals i.e. how they would like to feel and behave.
It is only when clients see this link that they are
motivated to work and change their irrational
beliefs. Again novice therapists often omit this
stage.

     During the re-examination stage of therapy,
rational-emotive therapists can use a variety of
cognitive, imagery, emotive and behavioural
techniques (Wessler and Wessler, 1980). When I
listen to the techniques that novice therapists
employ, I focus and comment on the following:
(1) I comment on the variety of techniques that my
supervisees employ over time. Here the greater the
variety of techniques that they have in their
armamentatium, the more likely they are going to be

successful in helping a broad range of clients. If therapists only use a limited range of techniques I try to ascertain the reasons for this. If therapists indicate that they only know a certain range of techniques, I often suggest others and model their possible applications. However, novices are often aware of other techniques but do not use them for other reasons. For example, one supervisee claimed not to use imagery techniques because she had great difficulty imagining events herself. My task here is to help supervisees identify and correct such blocks.

(2) I comment on my supervisees' skill at using particular techniques. Here I both directly comment on the way therapists employ the techniques and ask them to think of different ways of using them. I may model other ways of using such techniques or suggest to my supervisees that they listen to therapy sessions in the Institute for Rational-Emotive Therapy's tape library in which such techniques are skilfully demonstrated.

(3) I comment on the relevant use of particular techniques. Sometimes novice therapists employ techniques skilfully but inappropriately. Here supervisees often do not give enough thought to the use of techniques with specific clients with whom they are working. This danger is partially avoided if therapists adequately explain their rationale for using particular techniques and gain client cooperation beforehand. If clients cannot see a technique's relevance, this is one sign that perhaps it should not be used. In addition, therapists' choice of technique my be inappropriate for the modality of experience concerned. For example, if a particular client's irrational belief is manifested in imagery, then re-examination through verbal dialogue may not be as relevant as a carefully selected imagery method. Knowledge of clients' dominant modalities is important here.

The final cluster of tasks concerns the use of homework assignments. Homework exercises are important in rational-emotive therapy since their appropriate use helps clients to generalize their learning from the therapy situation to everyday experience. I listen carefully to the following:

(1) I focus on the amount of time that therapists devote to discussing possible assignments with their clients. A common fault here is that novice therapists devote too little time to this and consequently terminate the session by either unilaterally assigning homework exercises – a

procedure which often increases the possibility of client resistance - or by dropping the subject altogether. Here I usually ask my supervisees to consider how much time to devote to the process of assigning homework and monitor closely their performance on this parameter. (2) I focus on how adequately therapists prepare their clients for doing assignments. Important considerations here concern (a) the relevance of the tasks to the issues that have hopefully been thoroughly assessed and re-examined in the session in question; (b) clients seeing clearly the potential value of such assign-ments to their mediating and ultimate goals and (c) the clients being fully involved by therapists in the negotiation of homework assignments. (3) I listen carefully for evidence that therapists have tried to uncover possible obstacles to the successful completion of assignments by asking their clients in advance to speculate on what might stop them from carrying them out. If relevant information is uncovered by such enquiry, I listen to how therapists help their clients overcome such obstacles in the session. If this information is not asked for, I suggest to therapists that they think of the value of doing this routinely. (4) I listen for evidence that therapists engage clients in rehearsal of homework assignments either in imagery or using behavioural rehearsal in the session. This enables clients to gain some related experience of doing assignments and may in itself unearth further dysfunctional cognitions which might prevent clients from completing such tasks in their everyday situation. (5) I listen to the specificity of negotiated homework assignments. The more tasks have been specified, the more likely clients will be able to successfully carry them out. Finally, (6) I listen to the breadth of assignments suggested by therapists to their clients over the supervisory period. Preferably, if appropriate, a wide range of behavioural, emotive, written and imagery assignments should be used during therapy. If therapists are employing a narrow range of tasks, I try and discern the reasons for this and encourage them to think about remedying this.

In addition, throughout the supervisory period, I encourage my supervisees to encourage their clients to move towards independence so that they in fact acquire the skills to be their own therapists. If this is not done, I try and discover the reasons and encourage therapists to reflect on possible motivations that they might have for encouraging dependence. I attempt to sensitize my supervisees to the problem of client resistance to change and to possible reasons for this. Resistance may stem from client problems, therapist problems, poor therapist skills or their interaction.

Finally I endeavour to communicate my points to supervisees in the form of hypotheses for them to consider and possibly test. I encourage them to give me feedback on any suggestions that I have made and on my style of supervision in general so that I can fit the supervisory experience to individual supervisee requirements.

REFERENCES

The American Heritage Dictionary of the English
     Language. New York: American Heritage,
     1971.
Anchin, J.C., and Kiesler, D.J. (Eds.), Handbook
     of interpersonal psychotherapy. Oxford:
     Pergamon Press, 1982.
Arnkoff, D.B. Flexibility in practicing cognitive
     therapy. In G. Emery, S.D. Hollon and
     R.C. Bedrosian (Eds.), New directions
     in cognitive therapy. New York: Guilford,
     1981.
Bard, J.A. Rational proselytizing. Rational
     Living. 1973, 8(2), 24-26.
Beck, A.T. Thinking and depression: 2, Theory
     and therapy. Archives of General Psychiatry,
     1964, 10, 561-571.
Beck, A.T. Depression: Clinical, experimental,
     and theoretical aspects. New York: Hoeber,
     1967.
Beck, A.T. The diagnosis and management of
     depression. Philadelphia: University
     of Pennsylvania Press, 1973.
Beck, A.T. Cognitive therapy and the emotional
     disorders. New York: International Univer-
     sities Press, 1976.
Beck, A.T. Speculations regarding the biology
     of mental disorders. Unpublished paper.
     Centre for Cognitive Therapy, 1982.
Beck, A.T. Cognitive therapy of depression:
     New perspectives. In P. Clayton
     (Ed.), Depression. New York: Raven Press,
     1973.
Beck, A.T., and Emery, G. Cognitive therapy
     of anxiety and phobic disorders. Unpublished
     manual, Center for Cognitive Therapy, 1979.

References

Beck, A.T., Rush, A.J., Shaw, B.F., and Emery,
    G. Cognitive therapy of depression. New
    York: Guilford Press, 1979.
Beutler, L.E. Toward specific psychological
    therapies for specific conditions. Journal
    of Consulting and Clinical Psychology,
    1979, 47, 882-897.
Bordin, E.S. The generalizability of the psycho-
    analytic concept of working alliance.
    Paper presented at the meeting of the Society
    for Psychotherapy Research, Boston, June,
    1975.
Bordin, E.S. The working alliance: Basis for
    a general theory of psychotherapy. Paper
    presented at the meeting of the American
    Psychological Association, Washington,
    D.C., September 1976.
Burns, D.D. Feeling good: The new mood therapy.
    New York: William Morrow, 1980.
Carson, R.C. Interaction concepts of personality.
    London: George Allen and Unwin, 1969.
Coleman, R.E., and Beck, A.T. Cognitive therapy
    for depression. In J.F. Clarkin and H.I.
    Glazin (Eds.), Depression: Behavioral
    and directive intervention strategies.
    New York: Garland, 1981.
Dies, R.R. Group therapist self-disclosure:
    An evaluation by clients. Journal of Coun-
    seling Psychology, 1973, 20, 344-348.
DiLoreto, A.E. Comparative psychotherapy:
    An experimental analysis. Chicago: Aldine-
    Atherton, 1971.
Dombrow, R. On the use of early childhood material
    in rational-emotive therapy. Rational
    Living, 1973, 8(1), 17-18.
Dryden, W. Past messages and disputations:
    The client and significant others. Rational
    Living, 1979, 14(1), 26-28. (Reprinted
    here as Chapter 7).
Dryden, W. 'Eclectic' approaches in individual
    counselling: Some pertinent issues. The
    Counsellor, 1980, 3, 24-30. (a).
Dryden, W. Nightmares and fun. Paper given
    at the Third National Conference on Rational-
    Emotive Therapy, June 1980, New York. (b).
Dryden, W. Rational-emotive therapy and eclecticism.
    The Counsellor, 1982, 3(2), 15-22. (a).
    (Reprinted here as Chapter 8).
Dryden, W. Vivid RET. London: Institute for
    RET (UK), 1982. (b).

References

Dryden, W. The therapeutic alliance: Conceptual
     issues and some research findings. The
     Midland Journal of Psychotherapy, 1982,
     1, 14-19. (c).
Eisenberg, J.M., and Zingle, H.W. Marital ad-
     justment and irrational ideas. Journal
     of Marriage and Family Counseling, 1975,
     1, 81-91.
Ellis, A. Rational psychotherapy. Journal
     of General Psychology, 1958, 59, 35-49.
Ellis, A. Reason and emotion in psychotherapy.
     New York: Lyle Stuart, 1962.
Ellis, A. Growth through reason. Palo Alto,
     Calif.: Science and Behavior Books, 1971.
Ellis, A. Helping people get better, rather
     than merely feel better. Rational Living,
     1972, 7(2), 2-9.
Ellis, A. The rational-emotive approach to
     sex therapy. The Counseling Psychologist,
     1975, 5, 14-21.
Ellis, A. The biological basis of human irration-
     ality. Journal of Individual Psychology,
     1976, 32, 145-168.
Ellis, A. The basic clinical theory of rational-
     emotive therapy. In A. Ellis and R. Grieger
     (Eds.), Handbook of rational-emotive therapy.
     New York: Springer, 1977. (a).
Ellis, A. A garland of rational songs. Songbook
     and tape cassette recording. New York:
     Institute for Rational Living, 1977. (b).
Ellis, A. How to live with - and without -anger.
     New York: Reader's Digest Press, 1977.
     (c).
Ellis, A. Review of Beck, A.T. Cognitive therapy
     and the emotional disorders. New York:
     International Universities Press, 1976.
     Behavior Therapy, 1977, 8, 295-296. (d).
Ellis, A. Fun as psychotherapy. Rational Living,
     1977, 12(1), 2-6. (e).
Ellis, A. A rational approach to interpretation.
     In A. Ellis, and R. Grieger (Eds.), Handbook
     of rational-emotive therapy. New York:
     Springer, 1977. (f).
Ellis, A. Intimacy in psychotherapy. Rational
     Living, 1977, 12(2), 13-19. (g).
Ellis, A. Skills training in counselling and
     psychotherapy. Canadian Counsellor, 1977,
     12(1), 3)-35. (h).
Ellis, A. Rational-emotive therapy: Research
     data that supports the clinical and personality
     hypotheses of RET and other modes of cognitive

References

behavior therapy. <u>The Counseling Psycho-</u>
<u>logist</u>, 1977, <u>7</u>, 2-42. (i).
Ellis, A. Irrational ideas. In J.L. Wolfe
and E. Brand (Eds.), <u>Twenty years of rational</u>
<u>therapy</u>. New York: Institute for Rational
Living, 1977. (j).
Ellis, A. Toward a theory of personality.
In R.J. Corsini (Ed.), <u>Readings in current</u>
<u>personality theories</u>. Illinois, F.E. Peacock,
1978.
Ellis, A. Toward a new theory of personality.
In A. Ellis and J.M. Whiteley (Eds.),
<u>Theoretical and empirical foundations of</u>
<u>rational-emotive therapy</u>. Monterey, Calif.:
Brooks/Cole, 1979. (a).
Ellis, A. The theory of rational-emotive therapy.
In A. Ellis and J.M. Whiteley (Eds.).
<u>Theoretical and empirical foundations of</u>
<u>rational-emotive therapy</u>. Monterey, Calif.:
Brooks/Cole, 1979. (b).
Ellis, A. The issue of force and energy in
behavioral change. <u>Journal of Contemporary</u>
<u>Psychotherapy</u>, 1979, <u>10</u>, 83-97. (c).
Ellis, A. Rational-emotive therapy. In A.
Ellis and J.M. Whiteley (Eds.), <u>Theoretical</u>
<u>and empirical foundations of rational-emotive</u>
<u>therapy</u>. Monterey, Calif.: Brooks/Cole,
1979. (d).
Ellis, A. The practice of rational-emotive
therapy. In A. Ellis and J.M. Whiteley
(Eds.), <u>Theoretical and empirical foundations</u>
<u>of rational-emotive therapy</u>. Monterey,
Calif.: Brooks/Cole, 1979. (e).
Ellis, A. Rejoinder: Elegant and inelegant
RET. In A. Ellis and J.M. Whiteley (Eds.),
<u>Theoretical and empirical foundations of</u>
<u>rational-emotive therapy</u>. Monterey, Calif.:
Brooks/Cole, 1979. (f).
Ellis, A. Discomfort anxiety: A new cognitive-
behavioral construct. <u>Rational Living</u>,
1979, <u>14(2)</u>, 1-7. (g).
Ellis, A. Rational-emotive therapy and cognitive
behavior therapy: Similarities and dif-
ferences. <u>Cognitive Therapy and Research</u>,
1980, <u>4</u>, 325-340. (a).
Ellis, A. Psychotherapy and atheistic values:
A response to A.T. Bergin's "Psychotherapy
and religious values". <u>Journal of Consulting</u>
<u>and Clinical Psychology</u>, 1980, <u>48</u>, 635-
639. (b).
Ellis, A. The treatment of alcohol and drug

abuse: A rational-emotive approach. _Rational Living_, 1982, 17(12), 15-24.

Ellis, A. _The case against religiosity_. New York: Institute for Rational-Emotive Therapy, 1983. (a).

Ellis, A. The philosophic implications and dangers of some popular behavior therapy techniques. In M. Rosenbaum, C.M. Franks, and Y. Jaffe (Eds.), _Perspectives in behavior therapy in the eighties_. New York: Springer, 1983. (b).

Ellis, A., and Abrahms, E. _Brief psychotherapy in medical and health practice_. New York: Springer, 1978.

Ellis, A., and Becker, I. _A guide to personal happiness_. No. Hollywood, Calif.: Wilshire, 1982.

Emmelkamp, P.M.G., Kuipers, A.C.M., and Eggeraat, J.B. Cognitive modification versus prolonged exposure in vivo: A comparison with agoraphobics as subjects. _Behaviour Research and Therapy_, 1978, 16, 33-41.

Epstein, N., Finnegan, D., and Bythell, D. Irrational beliefs and perceptions of marital conflict. _Journal of Consulting and Clinical Psychology_, 1979, 47(3), 608-610.

Eschenroeder, G. Different therapeutic styles in rational-emotive therapy. _Rational Living_, 1979, 14(2), 3-7.

Eysenck, H.J. A mish-mash of theories. _International Journal of Psychiatry_, 1970, 9, 140-146.

Feldman, L.B. Depression and marital interaction. _Family Process_, 1976, 15, 389-395.

Frank, J.D. Psychotherapists need theories. _International Journal of Psychiatry_, 1970, 9, 146-149.

Freeman, A. Dreams and imagery in cognitive therapy. In G. Emery, S.D. Hollon, and R.C. Bedrosian (Eds.) _New directions in cognitive therapy_. New York: Guilford, 1981.

Garcia, E. Supervision of therapists. Unpublished lecture given at the Institute for Advanced Study in Rational-Emotive Therapy, New York City, July 11th, 1976.

Garfield, S.L. _Psychotherapy: An eclectic approach_. New York: Wiley, 1980.

Garfield, S.L., and Kurtz, R. A study of eclectic views. _Journal of Consulting and Clinical Psychology_, 1977, 45, 78-83.

References

Gendlin, E.T. Focusing. New York: Everest House, 1978.

Grieger, R., and Boyd, J. Rational-emotive therapy: A skills-based approach. New York: Van Nostrand Reinhold, 1980.

Hauck, P. Challenge authority: For thy health's sake. Rational Living, 1967, 2(1), 1-3.

Hoehn-Saric, R. Emotional arousal, attitude change and psychotherapy. In J.D. Frank, R. Hoen-Saric, S.D. Imber, B.L. Liberman, and A.R. Stone (Eds.), Effective ingredients of successful psychotherapy. New York: Brunner/Mazel, 1978.

Jones, R.A. Self-fulfilling prophecies: Social, psychological, and physiological effects of expectancies. Hillsdale, N.J.: Lawrence Erlbaum Associates, 1977.

Kassinove, H., and DiGiuseppe, R. Rational role reversal. Rational Living, 1975, 10(1), 44-45.

Kelly, G.A. The psychology of personal constructs. New York: Norton, 1955.

Knaus, W., and Wessler, R.L. Rational-emotive problem simulation. Rational Living, 1976, 11(2), 8-11.

Kovacs, M., and Beck, A.T. Maladaptive cognitive structure in depression. American Journal of Psychiatry, 1978, 135(5), 525-533.

Lazarus, A.A. Multimodal behavior therapy. New York: Springer, 1976.

Lazarus, A.A. In the mind's eye. New York: Rawson, 1978.

Lembo, J.M. The counseling process: A cognitive-behavioural approach. New York: Libra, 1978.

Mahoney, M.J. Psychotherapy and the structure of personal revolutions. In M.J. Mahoney (Ed.), Psychotherapy process: Current issues and future directions. New York: Plenum, 1980.

Maultsby, M.C., Jr. Help yourself to happiness. New York: Institute for Rational Living, 1975.

Maultsby, M.C., Jr. and Ellis, A. Technique for using rational-emotive imagery. New York: Institute for Rational Living, 1974.

Meichenbaum, D. Cognitive-behavior modification: An integrative approach. New York: Plenum, 1977.

Morley, E.L., and Watkins, J.T. Locus of control and effectiveness of two rational-emotive

References

therapy styles. Rational Living, 1979,
9(2), 22-24.

Nardi, T.J. The use of psychodrama in RET.
Rational Living, 1979, 14(1), 35-38.

Neuman, F. An eight-week treatment group for
phobics. Series of tapes and treatment
manual, 1982.

Raimy, V. Misunderstandings of the self: Cognitive
psychotherapy and the misconception hypothesis.
San Francisco: Jossey-Bass, 1975.

Reardon, J.P., Tosi, D.J., and Gwynne, P. The
treatment of depression through rational
stage directed hypnotherapy: A case study.
Psychotherapy: Theory, Research and Practice,
1977, 14(1), 95-103.

Rice, L.N. Therapist's style of participation
and case outcome. Journal of Consulting
Psychology, 1965, 29, 155-160.

Rice, L.N. Client behavior as a function of
therapist style and client resources.
Journal of Counseling Psychology, 1973,
20, 306-311.

Rice, L.N., and Gaylin, N.L. Personality processes
reflected in client and vocal style and
rorschach processes. Journal of Consulting
and Clinical Psychology, 1973, 40, 133-
138.

Rice, L.N., and Wagstaff, A.K. Client voice
quality and expressive style as indexes
of productive psychotherapy. Journal of
Consulting Psychology, 1967, 31, 557-563.

Rogers, C.R. The necessary and sufficient conditions of therapeutic personality change.
Journal of Consulting Psychology, 1957,
21, 95-103.

Sacco, W.P. Cognitive therapy in vivo. In
G. Emery, S.D. Hollon, and R.C. Bedrosian
(Eds.), New directions in cognitive therapy.
New York: Guilford, 1981.

Sager, C.J. Marriage contracts and couple therapy:
Hidden forces in intimate relationships.
New York: Brunner-Mazel, 1976.

Sharkey, P.W. Something irrational about rational-
emotive psychology. Psychotherapy: Theory,
Research and Practice, 1981, 18(2), 150-
154.

Shostrom, E.L. Actualizing therapy: Foundations
for a scientific ethic. San Diego: Edits,
1976.

Sluski, C.E. Marital therapy from a systems
theory perspective. In T.J. Paolino, Jr.,

and B.S. McCrady (Eds.), Marriage and marital
Therapy. New York: Brunner-Mazel, 1978.

Tschudi, F. Loaded and honest questions: A
construct theory view of symptoms and therapy.
In D. Bannister (Ed.), New perspectives
in personal construct theory. London:
Academic Press, 1977.

Wachtel, L. Psychoanalysis and behavior therapy:
Toward an integration. New York: Basic
Books, 1977.

Walen, S., DiGiuseppe, R., and Wessler, R.L.
A practitioner's guide to rational-emotive
therapy. New York: Oxford University
press, 1980.

Watzlawick, P. The language of change. New
York: Basic Books, 1978.

Weiner, I.B. Principles of psychotherapy.
New York: Wiley, 1975.

Weiss, R.L. The conceptualization of marriage
from a behavioral perspective. In T.J.
Paolino, Jr., and B.S. McCrady (Eds.),
Marriage and Marital Therapy, New York:
Brunner-Mazel, 1978.

Werner, E.E., and Smith, R.S. Vulnerable but
invincible: A study of resilient children.
New York: McGraw-Hill, 1982.

Wessler, R.A. The neurotic paradox: A rational-
emotive view. Rational Living, 1978, 13,
9-12.

Wessler, R.A., and Wessler, R.L. The principles
and practice of rational-emotive therapy.
San Francisco: Jossey-Bass, 1980.

Wessler, R.L. Direct and indirect influence
tactics in cognitive-behavior therapy.
Paper presented at symposium: When psychotherapy stalls: Behavioural guidelines
for responsible therapist action. Division
29, American Psychological Association,
87th Annual Convention, New York, September
4th, 1979.

Wessler, R.L. Alternative conceptions of rational-
emotive therapy: Toward a philosophically
neutral psychotherapy. Paper presented
at 12th European Congress of Behaviour
Therapy. Rome, Italy, September 5, 1982.
(a).

Wessler. R.L. Varieties of cognitions in the
cognitively-oriented psychotherapies.
Rational Living, 1982, 17, 3-10. (b).

Wessler, R.L., and Ellis, A. Supervision in
rational-emotive therapy. In A.K. Hess

References

(Ed.), Psychotherapy supervision, New York:
Wiley, 1980.
Wexler, D.A. A scale for the measurement of
client and therapist expressiveness. Journal
of Clinical Psychology, 1975, 31, 486-489.
Wexler, D.A., and Butler, J.M. Therapist modif-
ication of client expressiveness in client-
centred therapy. Journal of Consulting
and Cinical Psychology, 1970, 44, 261-265.
Whiteley, R.W. Depressive patients in therapy.
Midland Journal of Psychotherapy, 1981,
1, 9-13.
Young, H.S. Teaching rational self-value concepts
to tough customers. Paper presented at
the Third National Conference on Rational-
Emotive Therapy, New York, June 8, 1980.
Young, J.E., and Beck, A.T. Cognitive therapy:
Clinical applications. In A.J. Rush (Ed.),
Short-term psychotherapies for depression.
Chichester, Wiley, 1982.